Improving Primary Literacy

Improving Primary Literacy: Linking home and school provides primary teachers with practical answers to the following questions:

- How can primary teachers enlist the support of parents in helping children's literacy learning?
- How can teachers make use of the literacy learning that takes place in children's everyday lives outside school?
- What can parents do to support their children's literacy learning?
- How can teachers engage parents they find 'hard to reach'?
- How can teachers, parents and children share their different kinds of knowledge and understanding in order to improve children's literacy learning?

Using fascinating case studies of young children from a diverse range of family backgrounds, this book provides invaluable insights into the differing ways in which home and school literacy learning can be directly linked through home–school knowledge exchange activities and how this can be used to share knowledge between children, parents and teachers.

Tried-and-tested practical activities are included in the book, including: teachers and children making videos; parents and children taking photos; and information exchange through home–school folders and diaries. All of the activities have been shown to work in practice and can easily be fitted into the day-to-day activities of busy classrooms. Crucially, they will provide new ways for teachers to improve children's learning of literacy skills.

Anthony Feiler is a Senior Lecturer in Education, **Pamela Greenhough** and **Wan Ching Yee** are Research Fellows and **Martin Hughes**, is a Professor of Education at the University of Bristol, UK.

Jane Andrews is a Senior Lecturer in Education at the University of the West of England.

Mary Scanlan is a Senior Lecturer in Education at the University of Winchester.

David Johnson is a Lecturer in the Department of Educational Studies and Fellow of St Antony's College, University of Oxford, UK.

TLRP Improving Practice Series

Series Editor: Andrew Pollard, Director of the ESRC Teaching and Learning Programme

Learning How to Learn: tools for schools
Mary James, Paul Black, Patrick Carmichael, Colin Conner, Peter Dudley, Alison Fox, David Frost, Leslie Honour, John MacBeath, Robert McCormick, Bethan Marshall, David Pedder, Richard Procter, Sue Swaffield and Dylan Wiliam

Improving Primary Mathematics: linking home and school
Jan Winter, Jane Andrews, Pamela Greenhough, Martin Hughes, Leida Salway and Wan Ching Yee

Improving Primary Literacy: linking home and school
Anthony Feiler, Jane Andrews, Pamela Greenhough, Martin Hughes, David Johnson, Mary Scanlan and Wan Ching Yee

Improving Primary Literacy

Linking home and school

Anthony Feiler, Jane Andrews,
Pamela Greenhough, Martin Hughes,
David Johnson, Mary Scanlan and
Wan Ching Yee

Routledge
Taylor & Francis Group

LONDON AND NEW YORK

First published 2007 by Routledge
2 Park Square, Milton Park, Abingdon, Oxon, OX14 4RN

Simultaneously published in the USA and Canada
by Routledge
270 Madison Ave, New York, NY 10016

Routledge is an imprint of the Taylor & Francis Group, an informa business

© 2007 Anthony Feiler, Jane Andrews, Pamela Greenhough, Martin Hughes,
David Johnson, Mary Scanlan, Wan Ching Yee

Typeset in Melior and Futura by
Keystroke, 28 High Street, Tettenhall, Wolverhampton
Printed and bound in Great Britain by
Bell & Bain Ltd, Glasgow

British Library Cataloguing in Publication Data
A catalogue record for this book is available from the British Library

Library of Congress Cataloging in Publication Data
    Improving primary literacy : linking home and school / Anthony Feiler . . . [et al.].
      p. cm.
    Includes bibliographical references.
    ISBN-13: 978–0–415–36394–5 (pbk. : alk. paper)
    ISBN-10: 0–415–36394–2
    1. Language arts (Elementary)–United States. 2. Education, Elementary–Parent
    participation–United States. 3. Home and school–United States. I. Feiler, Anthony.
    LB1576.I48 2007
    372.6–dc22   2006032051

ISBN 10: 0–415–36394–2 (pbk)
ISBN 13: 978–0–415–36394–5 (pbk)

ISBN 10: 0–203–01514–2 (ebk)
ISBN 13: 978–0–203–01514–8 (ebk)

Contents

Series preface

The ideas for *Improving Practice* contained in this book are underpinned by high quality research from the Teaching and Learning Research Programme (TLRP), the UK's largest ever coordinated investment in education enquiry. Each suggestion has been tried and tested with experienced practitioners and has been found to improve learning outcomes – particularly if the underlying principles about Teaching and Learning have been understood. The key, then, remains the exercise of professional judgement, knowledge and skill. We hope that the *Improving Practice* series will encourage and support teachers in exploring new ways of enhancing learning experiences and improving educational outcomes of all sorts. For future information about TLRP and additional 'practitioner applications', see www.tlrp.org.

Preface

This book has arisen from the Home School Knowledge Exchange Project, a research project based at the Graduate School of Education, University of Bristol. Details of the project are presented in the Appendix.

The project team was large, and the authors of this book had different roles within the team. Anthony Feiler and David Johnson were co-leaders of the literacy strand of the project; Mary Scanlan was the teacher-researcher responsible for developing and implementing home–school literacy activities; Pamela Greenhough was leader of the project outcomes team, whose other members were Jane Andrews and Wan Ching Yee; and Martin Hughes was the overall project director.

For each chapter, one or two members of the team took the lead in preparing initial drafts, as follows:

Chapter 1:   David Johnson
Chapter 2:   Pamela Greenhough
Chapter 3:   Jane Andrews and Anthony Feiler
Chapters 4 and 5: Mary Scanlan
Chapter 6:   Anthony Feiler and Jane Andrews

Wan Ching Yee provided case study material for Chapters 2 and 3, and was involved in evaluating the activities described in Chapters 4 and 5. Pamela Greenhough redrafted Chapters 4 and 5, in order to clarify the distinction between activities suggested by the project team and activities actually carried out by the team. In addition, Anthony Feiler and Martin Hughes carried out an edit of the draft chapters, aiming to provide overall coherence while allowing the different voices of the authors to come through.

Finally, please note that we use the term 'parents' throughout the book as shorthand for 'parents and carers'.

Acknowledgements

The Home School Knowledge Exchange Project was funded by the Economic and Social Research Council (ref. no. L139 25 1078) as part of its Teaching and Learning Research Programme. We are very grateful to the Local Education Authorities of Bristol and Cardiff for their support, and to the many teachers, parents and children who took part in the project. We have used pseudonyms throughout the book and changed some details in order to protect the anonymity of the project participants. We would also like to thank the other members of the project team – Elizabeth McNess, Marilyn Osborn, Andrew Pollard, Leida Salway, Vicki Stinchcombe and Jan Winter – our project consultants John Bastiani, Guy Claxton and Harvey Goldstein, and our project secretary Stephanie Burke.

Chapter 1

Why link home and school learning?

This book is about the different ways in which children learn about literacy at home and at school. It is also about how these different ways of literacy learning can be brought more closely together, for the benefit of teachers, parents and children. The early chapters provide detailed accounts of home and school literacy learning as experienced by a small group of children. The later chapters provide practical examples of activities designed to bring home and school literacy learning more closely together, through a process of *home–school knowledge exchange*. We hope that readers of the book will gain new insights into the nature of literacy learning, and come to understand why home–school knowledge exchange is so important. We also hope that readers will try out some of the knowledge exchange activities for themselves, and invent new ones which are tailored to their own particular circumstances.

Two key ideas about children's learning

This book – and its companion volume *Improving Primary Mathematics: Linking Home and School* – are based on two fundamental ideas about children's learning and how it can be enhanced.

The first key idea is that *children live and learn in two different worlds – home and school*. Clearly, this is an idea that no one would seriously take issue with. Yet it is also one whose importance has never been fully accepted. When educators and politicians talk, as they frequently do, about the need to improve levels of children's literacy, they are usually advocating changes to the way children are taught literacy in school. This kind of literacy learning is of course very important: there is no doubt that much of what children come to know about reading, writing, and the nature of language takes place through their literacy lessons in school. But school is not the only place where literacy learning goes on. As we shall see in Chapter 2, children are also learning about literacy through their ongoing daily activities at home and in the wider community, as they interact with parents, grandparents, siblings and friends, as they play games, write messages and stories, or watch cartoons on TV. This kind of learning is often hidden from public view, but it is of vital importance in understanding how children come to be literate.

One consequence of children living and learning in two different worlds is that the two kinds of learning may become separated. Children may be unable or unwilling to draw on what they have learned in one world when they are in the other. The knowledge, skills and understandings they have acquired at school may not be accessible to them at home, and vice versa. Moreover, key adults who might be able to help children make the necessary connections between the two kinds of learning may not have sufficient knowledge to do so. Teachers may not know enough about what their children are learning at home, while parents may not know enough about what their children are learning at school.

In the area of literacy, this kind of separation seems to be particularly acute at the moment. In the UK, the teaching of school literacy has been transformed by the National Literacy Strategy. The literacy curriculum, the shape, content and pace of literacy lessons, the way that literacy is assessed – even the use of the term 'literacy' itself – are all very different from how many of today's parents were taught. As a result, parents may not feel sufficiently confident to help their children at home, or worry that they might be confusing their children if they try to do so. Similarly, the nature of many children's out-of-school lives may be relatively opaque to their teachers, particularly when the children come from a different ethnic or religious community to that of the teacher. In addition, the increasing prominence of popular culture in children's lives, and the role it has in shaping their ideas about literacy, may be something that their teachers are not fully aware of.

This brings us to our second key idea – *that children's learning will be enhanced if home and school learning are brought more closely together*. Again, this appears to be an idea that few would take serious issue with. Teachers have long been encouraged to draw on children's out-of-school interests in their teaching, and to keep parents involved with and informed about their children's learning in school. Parents have long been encouraged to support their children's school learning at home. And, indeed, there have been several influential research projects – some going back to the 1970s – which have demonstrated the value of parents and teachers working together to support children's learning, particularly in the area of literacy.

As with our first key idea, though, the importance of this second idea has never been fully accepted. Teachers and headteachers often tell us that the pressures they are currently under to 'raise standards' means that developing effective home–school partnerships is, for many of them, an area of relatively low priority. We would reply that the most effective way to raise standards is to bring together children's home and school learning. These are not two competing priorities: rather, one is the means to the other.

At the same time, we recognise that many teachers and headteachers are unclear about what methods they might use to link home and school learning. Unlike other areas of the curriculum, there is little clear guidance for teachers on what approaches and activities would most effectively bring this about. Nor are there many suggestions as to how to deal with some of the obstacles which might arise. This book and its companion volume *Improving Primary Mathematics: Linking Home and School* are intended to provide much needed guidance in this area.

The nature of this book

The book arises directly from a major innovative research project – the Home School Knowledge Exchange Project – which we carried out between 2001 and 2005. During this time we worked closely with teachers, parents and children from different communities in the two cities of Bristol and Cardiff, developing, implementing and evaluating a range of home–school knowledge exchange activities. We also carried out in-depth interviews with many of these teachers, parents and children, and asked parents and children to make videotapes of their home learning.

One strand of the project focused on home and school literacy learning for children in Years 1 and 2, and the book draws heavily on the work of that strand. At the same time, it is not intended to be a full account of the research and its findings (see the Appendix for more details of the project). Rather, it is an attempt to make project outcomes available in a usable form to all those interested in children's literacy learning – at all ages – and how it might be enhanced through home–school knowledge exchange. This includes:

- teachers
- headteachers
- literacy coordinators
- family learning coordinators
- teaching assistants
- students in initial training
- teachers on postgraduate courses
- teacher educators and other educationalists
- school governors
- parents and parents' organisations.

In order to make the contents of the book accessible to such a wide range of audiences we have deliberately emphasised practical action and the issues arising, and kept references to academic texts to a minimum. Readers are encouraged to try out and adapt the activities described here, and are free to photocopy and use the various sheets included in the text.

Chapter 2

Literacy at home

In this chapter, we look at some literacy events taking place in the homes of five children aged between five and seven years – Geraint, Seren, Luke, Poppy and Parveen. Through the exploration of these events, we will seek to establish some of the features and characteristics of what literacy can look like at home.

Events with literacy goals

Messaging

Geraint lives in a small terraced house with his mum, his dad who is a manual worker, his older sister, two younger siblings and a new baby brother. Geraint has a problem. He has recently been allowed to have a television in his bedroom but today he has been naughty and he has been told he can't watch it. It is coming up to 8 o'clock and he knows that his favourite 'soap', *Holby City*, is about to start. He loves watching the doctors doing the operations and the way the tensions are played out – will the patient live or die? When he got home from school, he checked the TV listings to make sure it was the right day. He is certain that it's on tonight. He thinks about going downstairs and saying he is sorry for being naughty but he knows this will get him into more trouble. The baby is asleep in his pram in the living room and Geraint knows that opening the squeaky door and pleading for a reprieve will annoy his parents, especially if the baby wakes up. He decides on a strategy that he often uses. He gets a scrap of paper and writes a note.

dear dad I'm sorry and please
can I have the TV on
circle yes or circle no

Geraint

   yes   no

as retold by Geraint's parents

Quietly, he creeps down the stairs and slides the note under the door. While he is waiting for a reply, Geraint goes into the kitchen and writes out his menu card for the following morning. Today, he writes:

I'll have plain toast and cereal.

Sometimes it's scrambled egg, but whatever he chooses, it will be different from what is written on his sister's menu card. His dad will use their cards to get their breakfasts ready for them the next morning.

Seren lives in a large terraced house in a slightly run down area with her mum, dad and older brother. She also has a problem. Yesterday, her first tooth fell out when she was running about in the playground at school. She didn't notice where it fell so, when she went to bed, she had no tooth to put under her pillow. She hoped that the Tooth Fairies would come anyway. She thinks that the fairies are always with you, like God, so they should know she has lost her tooth. But she awoke to disappointment – no coin under her pillow. It seems, after all, that the fairies don't know that she has lost her tooth. How can she let them know? Seren adopts the same strategy as Geraint. She decides to write a note. On a piece of paper measuring about three centimetres in each direction she writes:

to The toth feris
Mai toth ceim awt
and i nefor   p.
new so et got   t.
~~losst~~ lost   o.
from Seren

The 'p.t.o.' down the side of the paper is an afterthought, as, on the back of the note, she wants to include the date she lost her tooth. Her mum helps her to work out the date by getting the *Cute Baby Animals* calendar from the kitchen. On the back of the paper, Seren writes:

<u>15 Thursday</u>
Seren's
toth   pto

<u>of May</u>

When she has finished writing, Seren rolls up the note and places it in a tiny red velvet pouch, designed and sold (in a book called *My Tooth Fairy Book*) to hold lost teeth while they are under the pillow. That night, just before getting into bed, she rereads the note and adds '2003' after the word 'May', so there will be no confusion on the fairies' part as to the current relevance of the information contained in the note. Then she places it under her pillow.

In these two instances, we see examples of a form of home literacy event that we came across frequently on the Home School Knowledge Exchange Project, that is *messaging events*. These events were characterised by serving real purposes which were embedded in the social fabric of the children's lives. The purposes were the children's own and the children were the instigators of the events. The circumstances surrounding the events meant that there was also a genuine need for the use of writing. Written text becomes a more likely option when communication is to be made over a distance or over a period of time delay. Here, however, it was not distance or time that meant that writing was the preferred option. It was the fact that speech was ruled out by the situation. You cannot talk to a mythical entity who is present only when you are asleep. And you cannot speak with parents who have forbidden you to enter their presence.

The children were also aware of the audience for their literacy activity. Indeed, 'audience' is rather a passive description for the intended recipients of these notes, as it was the children's intention that their messages should galvanise active responses. Within the notes, we can see the ways in which the children were taking account of the reading of the notes by the addressees. Geraint has included the means of replying within his – a means of replying that will not disturb the baby provided that there is something to write with on the other side of the door. Seren shows her awareness of the future reading of her message by writing 'pto' on both sides of the paper. Imagine if the Tooth Fairies only read the back of the note.

The children also brought together in these messages aspects garnered from their varied experiences with writing and textual representations. Poppy, who lived with her mother and teenage brother, told us that she sometimes signed off the 'Sorry' notes that she threw through the window to her mother in the garden below (a common occurrence apparently) with 'I love U', using the representation popularised by mobile phone texting. Seren's note is also an interesting illustration of the ways children combine aspects of the literacy worlds that they are part of. Although her family is English speaking, Seren attends a Welsh medium school where all her literacy learning (and the rest of the curriculum) is conducted in the medium of Welsh. When she is at home, she almost always writes in English, i.e. the words are English words, as in her note to the Tooth Fairies. However, the representation of those words often utilises the sound-symbol correspondences from Welsh. The vowel groups in 'm*ai*', 'c*ei*m' and 'a*w*t' are all exact Welsh literations for the English sounds. Another example can be found in 'nefor' where /f/ is pronounced in Welsh like the English /v/. For 'Thursday' and 'May', Seren used other resources available to her and copied the words from the English calendar that was to hand after it had been used to check the date.

This blending of influences is sometimes referred to as *hybridity* or *syncretism* [📖 Reading 2.1 – see suggestions for further reading at the end of this chapter, page 20]. It shows that children are active, creative members of their literacy worlds. They draw on all manner of resources from the domains that they are simultaneously part of [📖 Reading 2.2] to enable their independence and to accomplish their goals.

Storying

Luke is in the same class as Seren. He lives in a large stylish terraced house with his father who is Welsh speaking, his mother and his older sister, Rhian. Luke does not often write at home. He prefers to 'be active' and spends hours out in the garden practising penalty kicks. Today, his mother, in an attempt to get him writing, suggests that he could make a list for a fantasy football team that he and his friends would like to play. Luke, however, is having none of this and holds up his hand in a stop gesture. He then announces 'A Little Naughty Man'. In answer to his mum's surprised question – 'What is a little naughty man?' – he draws and cuts out a little man with a triangle hat, helped throughout by his sister. He says it could have a string on it and be a puppet. His mum is still trying to get him writing and suggests he could make a list in his book of the things he would like to take on holiday or the things he would like to do at the weekend. But Luke wants his Naughty Man to be in the book and with the help of his sister sticks him on the front page with sellotape.

During the following 30 minutes, he fills the book with pictures and occasional captions as he tells the story of the Little Naughty Man. From the start, it is a violent and gory story. Mr Naughty Man stole diamonds, punched a man, lifted him up and 'throwed' him in a bin. He pushed a policeman down the stairs and made him bleed, took out a gun and shot him and the policeman died. At one point, there is a picture of a graveyard and rain, naughty rain which, when it comes, punches and kills people. On the story continues. Luke is wholly engaged in his narrative. When his mother makes suggestions that could lighten the story, e.g. 'When's Mr Nice Guy going to appear then?', he refuses them, adamantly asserting that it is *his* story not *hers*. When his mother suggests it is getting late and he should stop, he begs to be allowed to do 'just one more page'.

Luke's composition is surrounded by conversation mostly between his mother and sister. The conversation often takes the form of a commentary on what he is doing but it also ranges widely over aspects and features of stories and narratives.

Mum: He hasn't finished yet, there'll be a happy ending though
Rhian: I hope
Mum: I'm sure that.. because usually the good guys win, don't they, not the bad guys
Rhian: Yeh, *Scooby Doo*, they capture the person who dresses up like a ghost
Luke: *Titanic*
Rhian: Oh, *Titanic* (reconsidering)
Mum: *Titanic?* You haven't seen the *Titanic*, Luke

As seen on the video made by Luke's mum

Luke's contribution to the conversation here is small but highly significant – he has named a film which certainly does not have a 'happy ending'.

When Luke's mum leaves the scene from time to time, the story construction continues with Luke's sister playing a strong supporting role, sometimes suggesting ideas but also acting as immediate audience, modelling response to the story.

Luke: But Mr Naughty Guy is clever
Rhian: Oo, does he escape from jail or something?
Luke: He could walk through walls
Rhian: Aw
Luke: and, wherever you hide, he knows straight away
Rhian: Aw, is there any way you can hide so that he doesn't know?
         Is it.. is there something like an invention you have to build and he can never see you?
Luke: Well, if you hide in a dark closet, very dark,
         [1][you'll die
Rhian: [you'll be scared, will you be s..
         If you hide in dark
Luke: you'll die
Rhian: you'll die
Luke: In this story, you'll die
Rhian: [{so you have to come out}
Luke: [cos Mr Naughty spies {live} in dark
         And when you go in there
Rhian: So, wherever you hide.. and if it's dark where you hide, there's a spy hiding in there to kill you. Aw.
         (to the camera and the imagined audience behind it) so you'd better keep your lights on (little laugh) just in case he comes to your house and one of his spies catch you . . .
         Don't worry, it's just Luke's story (reassuringly)

Later in the video

We came across many *storying* events on the project. These included children writing stories but also drawing, telling, acting and even singing stories. Poppy, for example, sang out an exciting improvised version of *The Three Bears* when she was in the bath. (This came at the end of a video of her demonstrating her favourite dives.)

---

1 We use the following conventions in our transcripts:
  {word} shows some uncertainty as to what was said
  {. . .} unclear

  [
     simultaneous speech
  [

  .. a slight hesitation or change of direction in what is said
  . . . omission

On one occasion, Seren's mum came across her with her feet on the trampoline, her head and arms on the floor, writing a play script for the story of *Thumbelina*.

As with messaging, storying was owned by the children and they indulged in it for their own purposes and pleasure. Sometimes they retold stories, sometimes the stories were more newly made. And again, as with their messages, the children brought a range of influences and resources to bear on their stories. They built on and incorporated the knowledge they were developing from their experiences with the multiple story worlds they were encountering in books, comics, films, videos, DVDs and on television.

Dyson [Reading 2.3] refers to children appropriating and recontextualising symbolic material when they play, and suggests this is key to literacy learning in contemporary times. Some of this material may be from 'literary' sources as is possibly the case in Luke's use of 'the dark closet'. However, much of it derives from their experiences with popular culture. In the episodic, action-oriented structure of Luke's story, we can detect the influence of action movie sequences, and his book of pictures works like a storyboard for such a film. His story also relates to the 'scary movie' genre. At one point, Mr Naughty Man is dead and 'it's raining nasty blood, nasty blood is coming out of him'. In true scary movie plot style, Luke then announces, 'But he wasn't dead'. That children can develop a varied knowledge of narrative plotting and genre from their encounters with popular culture is also illustrated in Rhian's recognition of the formulaic in the endings of the *Scooby Doo* stories (where the frightening character always turns out to be someone dressed up as a ghost).

The influences from popular culture that contribute to children's understandings do not always come from first hand experiences of the original forms but have sometimes been mediated. If Luke's mother is correct, his use of the film *Titanic* (to refute her suggestion that stories usually have happy endings with the good guys winning) is not based on knowledge gained from actually watching the film. There are, however, other ways that such texts come to be known – as the video accompaniment to a hit song, for example – and incomplete as they are, these forms and the discourse surrounding them can also contribute to a child's growing literacy awareness. The elements of popular culture that get bound up in children's storying can also come second hand from other people. Luke's sister suggested that if she were doing this kind of story, she would write 'I'll be back', an allusion to the phrase used by Arnold Schwarzenegger in the film *The Terminator*:

Rhian: If I did one of those story.. in one of them I'd write 'I'll be back' (fiercely)
that sounds quite scary, doesn't it, 'I'll be back'
Luke: soon (quite fiercely)
Rhian: I'll be back soon to get you,
if he missed a shot and he went..
and the man he tried to shoot ran away,
maybe shouts 'I'll be back after you soon enough', and makes a big laugh again

Indeed, the reference here appears to be arriving third hand, since Rhian's easy acceptance of the addition of 'soon' to the phrase suggests that she has probably not seen *The Terminator* either. However, she has picked up on the expression's currency in action situations (possibly from playground games, etc.) and knows of its appropriateness for the genre. Influences from popular culture can be pervasive even when not experienced at first hand.

In our discussions with the children, we also found that the understandings about narrative that they were developing through their contact with pop-cult stories included knowledge about character. We gave them plastic figures and fridge magnets saved from cereal packets and Christmas crackers, that depicted fictional characters.

As the children unpacked and sorted them into sets, they named the ones they knew and chatted about them. Some of the characters, like those from the Walt Disney version of *Aladdin*, belonged to a single story. Others, like the Simpsons, were known in many different stories. These latter were particularly useful in discussion as they enabled conversations as to what the characters would typically do based on what they were like, as in the following interview with Poppy at the end of Year 2.

Int: I just wondered whether any of these you'd ever put in a story so.. let's just put them all out and you can have a look at them.

Poppy: (laughs) They look really funny. The Simpsons.

Int.   That one's from the Simpsons.

Poppy: And that one is too.

Int.   Do you know who that one is?

Poppy: That's .. I th.. that's Bart, I know that's Bart, and I know that's Maggie but I've forgotten what his name is.

Int.   Is he Mister.. Mister Burns is it?

Poppy: Yeah, Mister Burns that's it, that's Maggie . . . and that's Homer . . . and there's Bart . . . that's Marge, so they.. they're all the Simpsons, that's Lisa.. . . . .

Int.   What would happen in a Simpsons story, do you think?

Poppy: In a Simpson story, things like Mr Burns saying that Simpson can't have any money and that.. Maggie goes around following Marge all the time and.. then Homer takes Maggie out and Marge doesn't know where Maggie is but Mag.. Maggie's actually with Homer and em.. yeah stuff like that, and then with the Rugrats

Int.   Let's just think about Lisa as well, cos what kind of per..

Poppy: Yeah, yeah I forgot about Lisa

Int.   What kind of person is Lisa?

Poppy: I would probably . . . well with Lisa I'd probably like.. say.. I'd probably say that Bart likes going off skating and trying to jump over this thin.. sharks on his skateboard, real sharks, and Lisa saying – don't do it, stop it, why do you want to do it, you might get killed and stuff like that

Int.   So how come Lisa knows not to do it, do you think?

Poppy: Well because in the Simpsons, Lisa's really like sensible and stuff, so that's why.

Int.   Yes, she is, isn't she, and she knows quite a lot of stuff as well.

Poppy: Yeh, Marge and . . . them three know quite a lot, well Maggie can't speak at all so..

Int.   No but maybe she kind of joins with them.

Poppy: Maggie just walking around, just slides around everywhere.

Int.   Mm so do you think it's interesting that the ones that you say who know a lot, that's Lisa and Marge and Maggie, they're all the female ones.

Poppy: Yeah, yeah cos girls are sensible then boys, sensibler than boys.

The Simpsons characters were widely recognised by the children. Geraint described Homer as 'greedy and lazy' and explained how he had come to these conclusions:

> cos he keeps eating doughnuts and drinking stuff, and he's lazy 'cos he always sits down and never does nothing, he never goes to the {. . .} for the hotdogs, so Marge has to do it, and he only spins around in his chair when he's at work.

Seren described Homer as greedy and fat and said he 'loves doughnuts. Every time he sees them, he always eats them'. Characters from the *Winnie the Pooh* stories as represented by Disney were also extremely well known. Seren said of Eeyore, 'He's a very sad one and he talks like he's an old granny'.

Cartoons like the Simpsons were also popular viewing for Parveen, her two siblings and her many cousins. Parveen's family are Sikhs. Her father was 'born and bred' in the UK, her mother and grandfather moved to England from India and speak Punjabi most of the time at home. The family have cable TV and when Parveen's father goes off to work, the choice is between watching the cartoons favoured by the children or the Asian films favoured by their mother. Often the cartoon option wins. Parveen says she has learnt how to spell long words from watching the Simpsons and gives the example 'Congratulations' which she noticed written on a banner at a party given for Homer. Like the other children, she is developing a wealth of knowledge about character from her viewing. She is building an understanding of characters as more than one dimensional. This is especially the case with the Simpsons where the series itself plays with this feature.

Parveen: This is Lisa. She gets sometimes in trouble
Int: Does she do naughty things then?
Parveen: Well once she did because she cheated, well she wanted to go to the toilet and Bart said come to the boys' toilet, so she went in the boys' toilet and she found this boy who's Bart's friend called Nelson and he got the cheat for her maths test and she got them all right, but she didn't want to cheat but she took the paper and she started cheating and she said to herself when she went back home – what have I done? – and then she told her teacher that I've cheated, she said to her teacher that.. because her teacher said well done, Lisa, you got them all right, and she said to her teacher I didn't, I cheated and then em.. the principal of Lisa's school, he said to Lisa, what Lisa, you can't cheat cos you never ever cheat, you won't do a such a thing like that.

Popular culture, then, can be seen as providing a stimulating source of knowledge about narrative for children's emergent storying. However, this source may also provide cause for concern. Marsh and Millard [📖 Reading 2.4] have pointed out that many people feel uncomfortable with the ideologies which underpin many popular culture texts, ideologies which 'are often located in discourses of violence, racism, sexism, and other forms of oppression'. The violence of the action in Luke's story is unmissable. Indeed, it appears to be critical to his enjoyment and functions to drive the story writing onwards. Not only does he write about injury, killing and blood but he also seemingly delights in overthrowing the safe, ordered world. Policemen die. There is no escape – wherever you try and hide, Mr Naughty's spies will find you. Even the weather joins in (in a Shakespearean manner, cf. *King Lear*). There is something Bacchanalian about the disorder and Luke is the Lord of Misrule.

However, there are two interrelated aspects that should perhaps serve to reduce our anxieties about the violence. First, it is very clearly a fictional entity that Luke is working on. This is made more apparent by the conversations surrounding the drawing and writing (about possible endings, etc.) which underline its fictional quality. The recognition that it is 'just fiction' is also reflected in Rhian's comments like 'Don't worry, it's just Luke's story'. The second aspect is Luke's sense of control. He is in charge of the story rather than being subject to it. He is making choices and this is pointed up by the conversations around the story-making as to where he is taking it (e.g. whether it will have a happy ending). He is aware that he is engaged in a decision-making process. At the time of the *Titanic* conversation, he points out that he hasn't yet done the end. It may or may not have a happy ending. The two aspects (fiction and control) are related since the control is being exercised over a process of fiction making. Thus Luke says in the 'spies' conversation 'in this story, you'll die', suggesting that he is able to envisage other story worlds in which other decisions could be made. It is because the product is fiction that the choices are available. In addition, we should note that the violence in Luke's story does not go unchallenged. Both his mother and his sister indicate that it is not to their taste.

Documenting

After Seren wrote her note to the Tooth Fairies, she turned her attention to the *Tooth Fairy* book which had held the red velvet pouch. In it, there were pages on which the details of tooth loss and growth could be recorded. The following are examples of sections to be completed by the child:

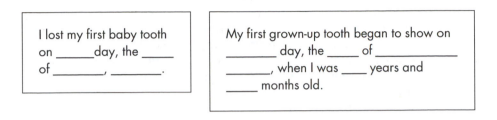

I lost my first baby tooth on _____day, the _____ of _____, _____.

My first grown-up tooth began to show on _____ day, the _____ of _____ _____, when I was ____ years and _____ months old.

She diligently filled them in, copying the calendar again for the date of loss of the baby tooth. When she started on the tooth appearance section, her mother turned back two pages of the calendar and showed her the day in March where the first showing of her grown-up tooth was already written down. Seren then used the information on this page of the calendar to record the details in her book.

As well as this commercial product that scaffolded the *documenting* of life's details, Seren had a diary. This was a book with hard covers and a lock on the side, which she used in a fairly free way without recourse to dates. At the beginning, there was a list of people's phone numbers. This included members of the family and friends from school. The next page was headed 'love birds' and underneath the title she had written a series of paired names, e.g. 'nanny loves Peter, Maisie loves Harry Potter'. Later in the diary, there was a list of the people invited to her birthday party.

The main feature of the diary was a piece that Seren had written to mark the death of her nan's dog, Rees. She explained it to her dad as follows:

> It's just a thing I writed in my diary because Nan's dog has gone to heaven, so I writed.. so I pretended that he writed a message. It's saying thank you for all the stuff that we gave him. (Reads) 'Hello, I'm in heaven. I just wanted to say thank you for the stuff that you gave me. Love Rees. And thank you for letting me go on the sofa and the bed'.

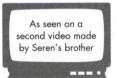

As seen on a second video made by Seren's brother

The entry was accompanied by pictures of the dog which had been cut from photographs and stuck in the diary. Underneath the writing was a drawing made to look like a print from a dog's paw. At the time of writing Rees' letter from heaven, Seren's favourite story-book was *The Last Polar Bears*. In this particular book, the narrative is created from a series of letters written by a grandfather to his grandchild about his adventures. Storying and messaging therefore come together in the book. The grandfather is accompanied on his adventures by a dog called Roo, who adds his paw mark to the grandfather's signature at the end of each letter. At the back of the book, there is a photograph of the author's dog, also apparently called Roo, with the real Roo's paw mark printed under his photograph to demonstrate his contribution to the creation of the book. In addition to the coming together of storying and messaging, the story world and the real world of the author are seen to come together within this book as well.

Seren seems to have taken from the book the idea of bringing together the real dog world with an imaginary dog world, and has created a product from that conjunction that uses make-believe messaging to act as a record of the dog's death. She also reuses the visual image of the paw print to represent the dog in her own text. Once again, we can see how features known from other contexts are brought to bear on the current event, to produce something new. The result here is a record or document that connects both to life and to other texts, although this intertextuality may not be immediately apparent. That the word 'text' derives from the Latin for web or weaving seems wholly appropriate here.

Seren's text is a charming and creative form of record that underscores the strength and flexibility of children's powers of adaption. However, it also shows that she is possibly not familiar with the stereotypical diary genre, or that of the obituary column, since neither of these modes informs her approach to the record of the dog's death. This should remind us that, while the home is a fertile ground in which children develop their knowledge of literacy, it cannot be comprehensive and their knowledge will be patchy and limited.

Events with everyday goals in which literacy is an incidental part

Cooking or 'Slushgate'

It's a Sunday afternoon at the end of June. Poppy is in the kitchen with her mum's boyfriend, Tom. They are making Flake Cakes for tea using a packet mix. They are at the point where they are combining the cake mix with the egg, water and oil, as per the instructions on the back of the packet. The next direction tells them to 'whisk on a slow speed'. The family don't have an electric whisk so Poppy is using a hand whisk and it is proving a bit difficult for her to keep the gadget turning. Tom reads aloud the next instruction on the back of the box 'and then on a high speed for two minutes'. He takes over the mixing, muttering to himself 'until thick and creamy'. Poppy suggests that he's mixing 'a bit too fast', so Tom hands the box to her so that she can tell him what it says.

From Poppy's video, set to record by her mum

Tom: From there
Poppy: (Reads) *Mix on a slow speed*
Tom: Slow speed, right (mixes extremely slowly)
Poppy: No, not that slow, Tom
Tom: Right (mixes very fast)
Poppy: No, Tom, on a slow.. look (reads) *on a slow speed*
Tom: Yeah
Poppy: *until com bin.. combined and then*
Tom: [*on a high speed*
Poppy: [*on high speed {for two}* (puts the box down)
Tom: Right next (looking at the box)
Poppy: (Picks up box) *On*
Tom: No, onto this one now (points to the next instruction)

The mixture is now ready to be poured into the cake cases. At this point, Poppy's mum arrives on the scene and questions the consistency of the mixture.

Mum: Are you sure you used the right mixture because it looks really runny, that shouldn't be that runny, and I know that
Tom: Shouldn't it?
Mum: No
Tom: (laughing) Do you think we're going to have a disaster area then?
Mum: They're really simple those, have you put the wrong mix in?

Tom:	[No I don't think so
Poppy:	[No (eating the mixture from the whisk)
Tom:	(stirring mixture) It's thick {and creamy}
Mum:	{Have you} done the right thing.. cos they're usually em.. it's more gooey, the consistency is more gooey . . . (picks up packet and looks in it)
Poppy:	{Gooey mixture} really nice {with them}, mmm, I love this (picking up some on her fingers and licking them)
Mum:	(Picks up the bag which previously held the mix)
Poppy:	Bit lumpy, Tom
Mum:	(Reads the bag) *Cake Mix* (Reads the back of the box) [*Combine the*
Poppy:	[{think} it's a bit lumpy
Mum:	*cake mix with the egg*
Poppy:	Done that
Mum:	You didn't measure out the water, did you?
Tom:	No
Mum:	You put too much water in, didn't you?
Tom:	Well I think that's {what may have happened}
Poppy:	Why didn't you measure out the water? (accusingly)
Tom:	Because I don't know what 15 millimetres [*sic*] looks like

As we can see, the goal here was to produce something edible for tea and literacy was *incidental* to the event. It was part of the means whereby the goal was achieved. If you were to ask Poppy what she was doing she would probably reply 'making cakes' (rather than reading). A significant proportion of literacy activity at home was like this, with an aspect or aspects of literacy being embedded in the unfolding of the event. Often, as here, the literacy side of things took the form of reading instructions. Other examples included making a model of a crossbow, making a model from the back of a cereal packet, doing DIY, planting seeds, playing board games and using a code from a Kinder egg to access a game on the Internet. Geraint's mum told how he would set up a reminder using a routine on their Digibox, so as not to miss another of his favourite programmes, the cartoon *Recess*.

It was clear that, in Year 1, Poppy already knew something about the direct and impersonal register of instructions (The National Literacy Strategy, Year 2, Term 1). At one point, she was waiting for the next instruction and mimicked to herself what she thought it would be. In a staccato voice which separated out each word, she enunciated 'Put the egg in'. In addition, she was building up her knowledge of the segmented and sequential nature of the instructional genre, as the reading of instructions was intermittent and punctuated by the cooking action. This was further reinforced by comments from Tom like 'onto this one now'. Since the reading was thoroughly embedded in the activity, it was also wholly meaningful.

However, reading the instructions was not limited to the simple purpose of directing the activity. It was also employed in the service of the other social purposes being played out in the event. It was used to create the comedy whisking routine. Tom needed the instructions to be read again, to make it clear that he was responding to them in an extreme manner – hence the handing of the box to Poppy so she would re-read the sequence. Poppy's mum used the retrospective reading of the instructions to try and establish where Tom and Poppy might have gone wrong and to add weight to her contention that the consistency was not right and a mistake had been made ('Slushgate' as Tom later referred to it). Her first go at error detection was to read the labelling on the discarded packet in the belief that the topping had been used instead of the basic mix. Subsequently, she looked at the instructions themselves. We find, then, the instrumental use of the text being combined with emotional reaction to the quality of the product. Impersonal as the writing of the instructions may have been, when used for real, the reading of the instructions is socially embedded and creates a variety of responses relating to a range of purposes.

I need an L, oh I've eaten it

Poppy's friend Ally has come round to play. They are having tea after a game of 'office workers', when they pretended to type letters, wearing sunglasses. Now they are eating sausages, cucumber, raw carrots and chips shaped like letters of the alphabet. They are laying out the chips on the table top to make words with them. Ally has made THE and Poppy has made YOU and ALL. Poppy wants to make Ally's name but needs another Y to add to her ALL.

Poppy: I'll swap for a Y
Ally: Yeah, you need one.
Poppy: (Gives Ally an N and receives a Y)
Ally: N
Poppy: (Licks the sauce off the Y. Places it on the table to make ALLY.)

Earlier in the day, before Poppy's bath-time diving demonstration

Poppy eats up Ally's name. She then decides that she wants to make the name 'Silas'. She puts out S and I.

Poppy: I've got no luh.. oh I've eaten..
Si luh (places two straight letters to make L)
Ally: Aa
Poppy: I've got no aa, you got an aa?
Ally: Nope
Poppy: Oh, Si lll.. Siless, eh . . .
Siluh (picks up letter E)
Sileh (puts letter down by word) Sileh, Si
That's an eh, Sileh, I'm doing an eh instead of an aa
Aw no, I've got no.. zuh
(picks up an N and places it on its side)
Silaz (little laugh)
(puts letters back on her plate)
That was meant to be a nuh
(picks up the N, turns it and eats it)

Here again, literacy is an incidental aspect of this event, as it was in the cooking episode above. However, here it is not the means whereby the goal is achieved but is more of an optional extra. That such a happening (eating a meal) has this literacy side to it is due to the ubiquity of script in the environment. The child's out-of-school surroundings are full of print. Even where letters might not be expected to be present, they can still crop up, as here, since they have become part of the design and decorating vocabulary associated with early childhood. Cathy Nutbrown noted of one very young child:

> Alex's bedroom curtains bore letters of the alphabet, as did her cot cover . . . Some of Alex's clothes were embroidered with logos, letters and captions, such as Baby, ABC, I love my Daddy.

> (Clough and Nutbrown, 2002, p. 48)

The mastery of this abundance of script can function as an important route for some children into the world of letters and meaning. One mother wrote in the literacy log of her son who was nearing the end of his time in Year 1:

> Read labels + notices around the house + outside – in fact, read almost anything except books, which he is still reluctant to do at home, though he pores over the illustrations for ages

What is noticeable about the tea-time event is the children's playful approach to the letters. Poppy responds flexibly to her set of material and extemporises with what is to hand. One letter is made to stand for another. An E functions as an A, and an N works as a Z which is itself a proxy for an S. The children's intentions are not limited by what they have. Once again, we see children's powers of adaptation in evidence as they use the resources available to improvise. Fun and their own interest drive the activity.

Events with literacy-learning goals

Reading with mother

Poppy is sitting on her bed next to her mum. It is Sunday evening and she is reading a book that she brought home from school on Friday. It is titled *A Proper Bike* and is from the *Oxford Reading Tree* series. When Poppy gets a word wrong, her mum helps her. The help is contingent. This means that at first only minimal help is offered which is then expanded if there is a continued lack of success in decoding the text. In the following excerpt, Poppy's mum indicates the location of the error by pointing to the word that has not been read precisely – 'showed'. Poppy continues to read it as 'shouted', so her mum homes in more closely on the error, asking, 'Where's the "t"'? Finally, when Poppy still fails to render it exactly, she provides the word for her:

Poppy: (Reading the following text on page 2 of the book: 'Biff and Chip came round to Aneena's.
They had a birthday card for Wilma.
'Happy birthday' they said.
Wilma showed them her new bike.
She polished the handle bars with her sleeve')
Biff and Chip came round to Aneena's. They had a birthday card for Wilma. Happy birthday they said, Wilma, shouted, them (restarts with the expression suggesting she thinks 'them' is the start of the sentence) *then, them,*

Mum: (Points to 'showed' which Poppy read as 'shouted'.)
What's that word?

Poppy: *shouted, shouted*

Mum: Where's the 't'?

Poppy: *Show* (pronouncing it like 'cow')

Mum: [*showed*

Poppy: [*shout, what?*

Mum: *showed*

Poppy: *Wilma showed them her new bike. She* (five-second pause) *polished*

Mum: Good

Poppy: *the handles*

Mum: *handle..*

Poppy: *with her.. handle bars*

Mum: Good

Poppy: *with her sleeve.*

Mum: Good

In addition to helping with the decoding, Poppy's mum's role includes providing positive feedback for accuracy and praise-giving. Very, very occasionally she makes a response to the story, for example a sympathetic 'Aw' when the character Aneena wishes she had a proper bike too.

This event represents the last category of home literacy events that we look at in this chapter. These are events where learning is to the fore and *literacy-learning* is the primary goal of the activity. Some of these events, as here, are at the instigation of the school. We can compare this event with others in which we have seen Poppy's involvement. There is a seriousness here on Poppy's and her mum's part. There is a sense that they are engaged in important business. The focus is on the child rendering a precise version of the text with as little help from her mother as possible. The tenor of the event is evaluative. That is not to say that it is negative. In fact, Poppy's mum is very positive in her praise. It is just that evaluating the nature of Poppy's reading is part of the agenda of the occasion. This contrasts with the reading that Poppy carried out when they were cooking, which was embedded in the activity and evoked no evaluative responses. But this is a reading-learning situation.

Henrietta Dombey, in a paper about the lessons children need to learn if they are to put reading to work for them and enrich their lives through it, has argued that children need to talk about the text they read. She writes:

> Children need to talk about the text they read, interpreting and commenting on the events, facts and characters, and relating them to those they know from their own first hand and second hand experience. They need to express and share their enjoyment, pleasurable fears, puzzlement and pondering, the sources of so many of the important meanings they will make from books. This companionship should be generous, allowing and encouraging children to make their own meanings, but extending and challenging those that are narrow or at odds with the text.
>
> (Dombey, 1995, p. 27)

In her paper, Dombey was discussing the several roles that a reading teacher might aim to play at school to support learning. Here she was describing that of a reading companion. Teachers may hope that such reading companionship will also be provided by parents when they get them involved in reading school books with their children at home. However, when Poppy read her book with her mum there was no such discussion about the story. In some of our previous research [☐ Reading 2.5] we found a wide variation in the amount and nature of discussion or 'conversing' that parents engaged in when their children read with them. On this occasion, Poppy's mum behaved in ways that were similar to the 'low conversers' in our earlier study. For example, she did not elicit Poppy's responses to the story that she had just read nor did she make any connections between the text and Poppy's life. This contrasts with an occasion when Luke was also reading a book from the *Oxford Reading Tree* series at home. At the end of the story *Car bach gwyllt* (*The little wild car*) his sister started to make links between the story he had just read and their own experiences:

Rhian: Was it a bit funny? Is it like me and you fight sometimes?
Luke: Yeah
Rhian: When Dad buys us a toy and you want it but I want it, we start fighting, and Mum and Dad go 'oh no'
Luke: And I pull your hair like that
Mum: So the story is similar to how you two are

Here, the direction of the connection being made is from life to text, bringing the experiences of life to the understanding and appreciation of the reading. On another occasion, the direction was from text to life, as the family discovered that the cause of the awful smell emanating from Luke's room was the potion he had made in the style of *George's Marvellous Medicine* in an attempt to make himself as clever as his older sister.

Learning with grandfather

Parveen attends Punjabi lessons at the local gurdwara (temple and community centre) on Wednesdays from four o'clock to half-past seven. As a Sikh, she is learning to write Punjabi in the Gurmukhi script. This is a syllabic alphabet which means that all consonants have an inherent vowel. The vowel is changed by the use of diacritics which are additional signs, like accents, that are written before, after, above or below the consonant. The script also contains more consonants than the Roman alphabet. It can be a challenge to learn. Parveen's father spoke about reading Punjabi in the following way:

> Again I can't read as well in Punjabi – very hard. Not so much hard but these are very hard learning, because older word styles, learning spellings.. again I didn't get the opportunity or sometimes I did go for it but didn't succeed on that so..

However, Parveen has help in the shape of her grandfather who has strategies for helping her remember the letters. Here she is chatting to her dad about the alphabet and her grandfather's help:

> I can say all of them. Urha, erha, eerhi, sussa, haha, kukka, khukha, gugga, ghugga, ungga, chucha, chhuchha, jujja, jhujja, nenya, tainka, thutha, dudda, dhudda, nahnha, tutta, thutha, duda, dhuda, nunna, puppa, phupha, bubba, bhubba, mumma, yaiyya, rara, lulla, vava, rahrha. These others, five extra ones, shall I say them? Shusha beri bindi sarboleh. Khukha reli bindi karpoleh. Gugga beri bindi karpoleh. Chucha beri lindi charpoleh. Fuffa beri bindi farpoleh. And I know how to them off by heart, which I did. And my fa.. because my grandfather learnt me how to – off by heart. And when I first learnt them, I did it like this, I did it five at a time so I did the first five and then the second five, that makes ten. Then I did the second five and the second five, the second five, yeah. Then I got on and on and on and then, I got to the end and I got.. reminded it in my head and I got.. learned so far and I'll tell you how I learned that, I learned it.. sometimes I go to.. sometimes I learn by my um.. grandfather which does a test. Because I know it off by heart and it's really good to learn it.

The separation of the letters into groups of five is a traditional way of dividing up the total and the sets reflect the way the sounds are made. For example, the members of the second set – kukka, khukha, gugga, ghugga, ungga – are gutterals. Grandfather's assistance was much appreciated by Parveen who had found it 'scary to do it' at first, 'because I couldn't keep them in my head'. In addition to learning to write in Punjabi, Parveen is also learning about language in general and its representation. She knows, for example, that 'the Indian alphabet has got more letters than the other alphabet'.

Literacy as social activity

We are nearing the end of this look at some home literacy events. Before we leave them, there are a couple of further aspects we would like to highlight. First, it is striking just how 'peopled' these events have been. As well as the five children we have focused on – Geraint, Seren, Luke, Poppy and Parveen – we have also met their siblings, parents, extended-family members, playmates and parents' friends. Once we step outside the home, we find still more people involved in the children's literacy experiences. As with events within the home, the involvement of others may be specifically aimed at the learning of literacy, as when Parveen attends the gurdwara to learn to read Punjabi with the teachers there. It may, on the other hand, also occur incidentally as a part of other activities. Seren, for example, goes to judo classes and in a photograph she is shown standing by a banner with Japanese writing on it. She has learnt from her teacher (or Sensei), that the symbols say 'circular movements'. Indeed, she has also learnt from her judo teacher to use the word 'symbol' in this context.

We can see, then, that many different people can be involved in children's experiences around literacy out of school. And this involvement can take different forms. Within these interactions, the role of the child is not fixed but may vary across and within occasions. The child is novice and knower, helper and helped. Geraint occupies a middle position in his large family. Sometimes his older sister, Meg, reads books with him:

Meg: I help him to break it down, don't I, Geraint?
Geraint: Yeah cos I was..
Meg: And after we've read a page I ask him questions and he looks through.. easy questions, like what is the Captain's name and he'd say Captain Flint and I . . .
Geraint: But he's dead now
Meg: The one you hate and if.. I ask him what.. um.. what that name, he goes to the front like that, and he says..
Geraint: Moore
Meg: Moore, he finds out the names or the..
Geraint: You asked me what that man's name is and it's John Silver
Meg: Yeah, that's right

At other times, however, it's Geraint who is in charge as when he reads to his younger brother. This happens most evenings as it's Geraint's job to help his brother get off to sleep and he uses reading as the means.

Box 2.1

How might teachers find out about out-of-school literacy events?

Some of the teachers involved in the Home School Knowledge Exchange Project wanted to find out more for themselves about the literacy events the children in their classes engaged in out of school. They asked the parents and children to keep *literacy logs*.

Poppy's teacher sent home a letter that listed some of the kinds of activities that might be included in such a log – sharing a story, reading and writing cards and letters, reading books, magazines and comics, reading signs and labels, playing games and following instructions for making things. She asked the parents to keep a record of the literacy events undertaken with their child.

Geraint's teacher wanted a less wordy, more 'user-friendly' format. The sheet she used is shown here as Photocopiable sheet 2:1 (see page 21).

In trying to gather this kind of information from parents, it can be difficult to balance the need to be supportive (and give them some idea of what is being

continued

> sought) with the desire not to restrict or limit their responses. It can help here to think through what will be done with the information.
>
> It will also be important to consider how to avoid such requests for information sounding as though this is snooping. Poppy's teacher wrote that she wanted to build on the things that the children did at home, in the classroom.

In this chapter, we have explored just a few of the ways children are learning about and using literacy out of school. In their activity, we have seen that literacy is much more than decoding or encoding print. It is also about the way it fits into and promotes social ways of being.

Further reading

📖 *Reading 2.1*

Eve Gregory, Susi Long and Dinah Volk have brought together a series of studies they refer to as Syncretic Literacy Studies. These describe the ways children syncretise (bring together and blend) the languages, literacies, narrative styles and role relationships of the groups they belong to, and from this create new forms.

Gregory, E., Long, S. and Volk, D. (2004) *Many Pathways to Literacy: young children learning with siblings, grandparents, peers and communities*, London: RoutledgeFalmer.

📖 *Reading 2.2*

Central to the process of syncretism is the recognition that children are *simultaneously* members of different groups or worlds which are not kept separate. Charmian Kenner has explored this area working with bilingual children.

Kenner, C., Kress, G., Al-Khatib, H., Kam, R. and Tsai, K.-C. (2004) 'Finding the keys to biliteracy: how young children interpret different writing systems', *Language and Education*, 18: 124–144.

📖 *Reading 2.3*

Anne Haas Dyson has written widely on the importance of materials from popular culture in children's literate activities. In this easily accessible paper, she traced children's appropriations back to their non-academic sources in animation and computer games and tracked 'their academic fates as children wove them into varied school defined practices'.

Dyson, A. H. (2002) 'Textual toys and compositional tutus: studying child literacy in the context of a child culture', invited key note address given at the inaugural session of the ESRC seminar series on *Children's Literacy and Popular Culture*, Sheffield. Available online at www.shef.ac.uk/literacy/.

📖 *Reading 2.4*

In their book on literacy and popular culture, Jackie Marsh and Elaine Millard discuss ways of approaching and using popular culture texts in the classroom. In their second chapter ('Challenging racism, sexism, violence and consumerism'), they recognise that popular culture can be infused with unappealing messages and that these can form a barrier to teachers' building on children's interest in popular culture in school. They suggest ways in which the messages can be challenged whilst still allowing the texts a presence in school.

Marsh, J. and Millard, E. (2000) *Literacy and Popular Culture: using children's culture in the classroom*, London: Paul Chapman.

📖 *Reading 2.5*

In a study carried out before the implementation of the literacy hour, we videoed 32 children reading with a parent at home and with their teacher at school. We found differences across parents in the way they interacted with their child around the book. Some talked about the text, others did very little of this and concentrated on decoding. Teachers were especially likely to include episodes of discussion. We called the talk conversing and found that it took four main forms – responding to the text, labelling and identifying, priming the child as to the content of the upcoming text and making sense of what was being read.

Greenhough, P. and Hughes, M. (1998) 'Parents' and teachers' interventions in children's reading', *British Educational Research Journal*, 24: 383–398.

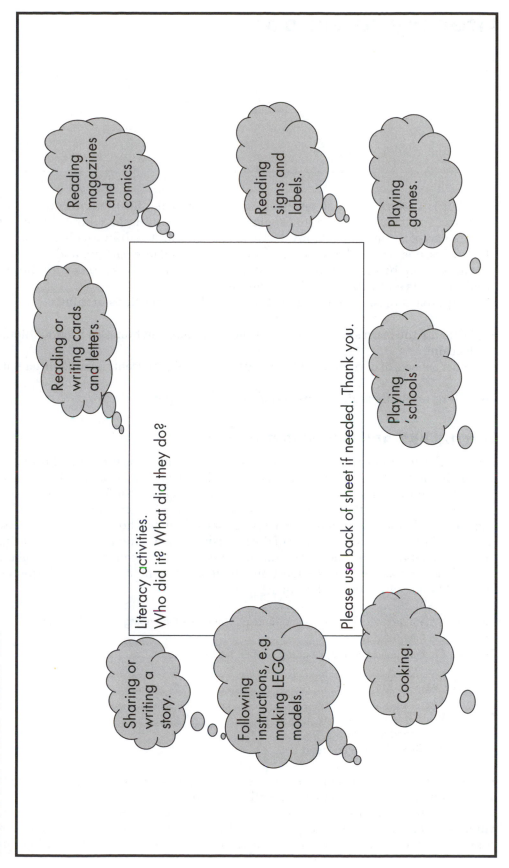

Chapter 3

Literacy at school

So, what is literacy teaching and learning in school like for the children we read about in Chapter 2? This chapter explores literacy learning in school through the experiences of Seren, Luke, Poppy, Parveen and Geraint. We draw on observations of literacy lessons where these children and their classmates participated in literacy activities set up by their teachers. We also draw on our conversations with the children's teachers and with the children themselves.

We approach these school literacy lessons with two questions in mind:

- What are the main similarities and differences between home and school literacy learning?
- What aspects of current school literacy teaching might parents be unfamiliar with?

We will return to these questions at the end of the chapter.

Seren, Luke and the postcard lesson

Seren, Luke and their classmates sit on the carpet facing their teacher, who sits on a low chair. Next to her is a stand with a large book placed on it. The book is *A Monster of a Joke* and the class have been working on it during the last few lessons. Like all lessons in this school, the literacy lesson is conducted in Welsh: however, we will use English translations here. (It is worth noting that although schools in Cardiff follow a literacy scheme that shares aspects of the English National Literacy Strategy, teachers in Wales generally have more choice on curriculum content than teachers in England.)

The teacher asks the children questions about the cover of the book and the pictures inside. At one point she asks Seren:

Teacher: Where are these children going, Seren? Where are they going to? To the zoo?
Seren: On their holidays
Teacher: On their holidays. They're going on their holidays

Later she asks Luke:

Teacher: What is Mum doing here, Luke?
Luke: She's reading a book
Teacher: Reading a book. Very good

The teacher also asks the children to read aloud together various sentences from the book. Seren and Luke join in with the other children.

The teacher elicits from Seren that two of the characters in the book – Onw and Mum – are going to buy a postcard to send to Dad. She brings out a card with the words 'a postcard' on it and asks several children to repeat the word 'postcard'. She then discusses with the children whether they have sent postcards in their out-of-school lives and what they might write on them. Luke makes a suggestion:

Luke: When you send a postcard you can say what you're doing
Teacher: Excellent. You can say what you're doing

At this point the teacher produces two postcards which she has received from friends in Australia, and tells the class what is written on them. She elicits from the children several suggestions about what the characters in the story might write on their post-cards, and then continues with the story. At different times she reads the story herself, asks the children to read aloud together, and discusses with them the pictures and the plot. Eventually she puts the book away and says:

Teacher: We're going to stop reading the book. We're going to look a bit more at these postcards

After some more discussion with the children about the nature of postcards, she asks again what the children in the story might write on their postcard. One child suggests 'We are in Scotland'. The teacher points to the flipchart on the other side of her and asks:

Teacher: Who can write 'Scotland' for me on the flipchart?
              (Seren raises her hand)
Teacher: Right, Seren, come on out
              (Seren goes to the flipchart)
Teacher: Right. Seren is going to write 'Scotland'. Move back. Now, will you all write the first capital letter in the air for me to see. (this is an A in the Welsh word for 'Scotland') A – are you trying? Not at all? Will you look up? Right. Say the word 'Scotland' to help Seren

              (The children all chant the word 'Scotland'. Seren finishes writing, gives the pen back to the teacher and returns to her space on the floor.)

The teacher tells the class that the word 'Scotland' is given the definite article in Welsh (as in French). She then asks for other suggestions for the content of the postcard, and asks children to write these suggestions on the flipchart. Luke suggests 'we are having a good time' and the teacher writes this up herself. Finally the postcard is finished and the children read it out together:

> *Dear Dad, we are in Scotland. We are having a good time. Cad and I are fishing. Love from Onw.*

The teacher suggests that Onw would send Dad a kiss at the bottom of the card, although a few boys greet this suggestion with looks of disgust.

For the final stage of the lesson, the children break into four groups. Museum group stay on the carpet and play a game of Pelmanism with some flashcards, Library group write their own postcards on small individual whiteboards, Castle group read a leaflet and answer some questions on a worksheet, and Town Hall group do some cutting and sticking. Seren and Luke are both in Museum group and their teacher hands them some flashcards. Seren distributes the cards around the floor. The group members choose cards and discuss what to do. The teacher asks Seren what's happening:

Seren: Yes, everyone's had them

Luke gets into an argument with another boy. He goes to tell the teacher and she comes over to sort it out. The teacher decides – on the basis of another girl's testimony – that Luke is in the wrong and tells him:

Teacher: You play fair or not at all

The group settle down to their game. After 15 minutes the children are asked to stop and move into the next space in the room in order to work on the activity that has been set up there. For Museum group this means they are now writing their own postcards on individual whiteboards. However, Seren only manages to complete one line on her postcard before it is time to move on again.

Reflections on the postcard lesson

The postcard lesson illustrates several features of literacy lessons which have recently become prominent in England and Wales. For example:

- The lesson, which lasts nearly an hour, is devoted almost entirely to aspects of reading and writing – the 'literacy hour'.
- Much of the lesson is focused on a large book – the 'Big Book' – which is set up at the front of the class so that all the children can see it and read the words in it.
- The lesson was carefully planned by the teacher and has a clear structure, with three main phases – whole class work on the Big Book, whole class work on the postcard, and activities in smaller groups.
- The teacher uses a range of teaching techniques to involve as many children as possible in the lesson – 'interactive whole class teaching'.

The teacher told us she was 'very confident' about teaching literacy, and that it was 'one of my favourite things'. She also said that she enjoyed the structure of the literacy hour, and had found it 'very successful'. She thought that in a Welsh-medium school it was particularly important to develop the children's accuracy in their use of vocabulary and grammar, and that these provide the basis for children's developing literacy skills:

> They have to be fed so much more in our school – vocabulary, sentence pattern, sentence structure. And to be able to practise this they need to be given a lot of situations, many situations, where this can work, such as role-play . . . working with puppets, talking to adults, talking to other people. Again, it doesn't happen as much as I think it should because of what you have to achieve with the curriculum.

The postcard lesson also provides some interesting comparisons with what we called 'messaging activities' in Chapter 2. There we saw Seren writing a message to the tooth fairy and Geraint writing to his parents to ask if he could watch TV. In both cases there was an expectation that the messages would be read and a tangible result would occur: a coin for Seren and permission to watch TV from Geraint's parents.

Much of the postcard lesson also centres on the 'messaging activity' of writing a postcard. During the lesson the teacher successfully elicits some of the children's own out-of-school experiences of writing and receiving postcards, and she introduces two postcards she has received from friends in Australia. She also engages in extensive discussion with the children about both the content and form which a postcard might take. At the same time, the actual activity of writing a postcard in school does not seem to have an authentic purpose. Once the children in Library group have finished writing the postcards on their whiteboards, the writing is then wiped off so that the next group can continue the exercise. Unlike the messaging activities at home, these are postcards without readers and without respondents. This may explain why Seren, who engages so creatively and prolifically in writing at home, manages only to complete one line of her postcard before she is moved on to the next activity.

This raises the issue of how time is managed in school-based literacy learning. In the postcard lesson the amount of time which different groups spent on different activities is controlled by the teacher and seems to be motivated by an organisational principle (making sure children have a go at each activity), rather than by a judgement of whether a piece of work is finished or not. This teacher-timed style of engaging in literacy contrasts strongly with, for example, Luke's experience of negotiating with his mother to allow him to complete 'one more page' of his Mr Naughty Man story. Indeed, this lack of control over his time was something that Luke himself pointed out when asked if he would like literacy teaching at home and school to be 'more similar'. Luke's reply suggests that he appreciates the way he can work at his own pace at home, even if this is rather a slow pace:

> Yeah, cos in school it's normally she tells us a lot of stuff to write about films and stuff, and it's boring cos she didn't let us have a break, cos normally I just do some writing and then go and watch some TV, and then next day I just relax . . . and I add to things . . . it takes months to do my book thing.

Poppy and the desert lesson

Poppy is sitting on the carpet with the rest of her class, facing her teacher. They are looking at a non-fiction Big Book about deserts which was first shown to them the previous day. The teacher asks the children what was the 'most interesting' thing they found out from the book. One child suggests 'there are five seasons'. The teacher prompts them with a more specific question:

Teacher: What about the flowers?
Poppy: It's about the cacti, they can live in winter

The teacher asks individual children to read aloud from the pages covered the previous day. Then the whole class read together some of the new sections. The teacher orients the children to the way in which the text is laid out for a particular purpose, explaining that: 'We'll read the large text first as that is the main bit of information.' The class read aloud the following text together:

Children: Like desert plants, the animals have made amazing adaptations

The teacher explains that 'adaptation' is a 'tricky word' and asks the class, if they adapt what have they done? The children are unsure, so the teacher re-reads the sentence. One girl suggests 'learnt how to store water', but the teacher explains it as 'changing'. The class continues reading aloud from the Big Book, and the teacher tells them that by reading the book they will develop ideas about how to be well-organised in their own writing.

After a while the teacher takes over the reading herself. She asks the children to tell her what was interesting in what she read. The section includes some information about the roadrunner bird, which can run at speeds up to 15mph. One boy makes a comparison between the roadrunner and a motorbike. The teacher says this would be a good comparison to include: a motorbike goes faster than 15mph so this would be a good use of information.

In the next stage of the lesson the teacher tells the children they are to write an introduction to a piece about deserts. She sticks an evocative picture of a desert scene on the board. She asks the children to 'tell someone close to you what you think would be good information to include'. Poppy gets into a group with four other girls to discuss what they might do.

After a while the teacher asks one of the girls to suggest a sentence. Her suggestion is: 'as the sun sets, some animals arise'. The teacher obtains other suggestions from other children and makes a compilation of these suggestions on the board:

As the sun rises some animals rise, because it is much cooler for them cactuses bloom now the heat of the day would be too hot and they wither bloom

The teacher asks the class whether this makes sense and what punctuation is needed. After some discussion the writing is amended as follows:

As the sun sets some animals rise, because it is much cooler for them. Cactuses bloom now. The heat of the day would be too hot and they would wither. bloom

(The word *bloom* is repeated at the end as one child has suggested it should be in a glossary.)

In the final stage of the lesson the teacher produces some sheets which show four pictures – a cactus, lizard, butterfly and dragonfly. She explains that 'your job is to write captions to go with these'. She says they will need to make the captions interesting, and explains that the audience for their writing will be their soon-to-be Year 3 teacher (who has joined the class) and the researcher who is carrying out the observations. The children work in pairs for this task – some chosen by the teacher and some not.

Poppy works with one of her friends. She holds the pencil and writes in a very small, neat script. By the end of the lesson she has written at least two sentences for most of the pictures, but nothing for the dragonfly. The lesson finishes early because the children are to attend a talk on recycling, and there is no time for a plenary.

Reflections on the desert lesson

Like the 'postcard lesson' described earlier, the 'desert lesson' shows several distinctive features of how literacy is currently taught in schools. The lesson is clearly structured and proceeds through a number of pre-planned stages. The children work mostly at whole class level although in the final stage they work in pairs. The central focus for the whole class work is another 'Big Book', which is used to support a range of literacy activities: these include reading aloud by the teacher, by the whole class, and by individual children. Unlike the postcard lesson, though, the Big Book used here is non-fiction rather than fiction. Poppy's views on this emerged in the extract below:

Interviewer: How do you feel about the Big Book reading?
Poppy: I like the Big Books
. . .
Int: Some people just like reading stories and other people they like to read like about ships and aeroplanes and animals and places..
Poppy: I don't like.. what is it? Is it non-fiction or fiction, not stories?
Int: Well, the stories are fictions and the other things..
Poppy: OK, I don't like non-fiction

Another difference between the desert lesson and the postcard lesson is that Poppy's teacher was more ready to provide the children with overt purposes for their literacy activities. At one point, for example, she tells them that reading the Big Book will help them when they subsequently start planning their own writing. Later she is careful to provide an intended readership for the writing the children are producing at the end of the lesson, that is, their next teacher and the researcher. The approach adopted by Poppy's teacher, where literacy is woven into other curricular activities (in this example, finding out about deserts) and where literacy is viewed as a means to an end, ties in with research into effective teaching reported by Kathy Hall [📖 Reading 3.1].

Poppy's teacher was ambivalent about the National Literacy Strategy. She said:

> I think it's very supportive for new teachers . . . But having said that I think it's been quite negative in other ways in terms of being too much of a straightjacket, so that some of that creativity and responsiveness to children's interest died along with it. Because you have to do instructions two weeks, and then six weeks later you'd come back to instructions, whether you got them or not.

It was also clear that her own practice was not constrained by the Strategy:

> Well, I have to say I've hardly looked at the Literacy Strategy all year and actually, if I were being monitored in terms of coverage, I haven't a clue really whether I've done the correct number of weeks on each thing, because [name of head teacher] keeps saying she wants us to be risk takers and to try things differently. So we've much more gone with what the children want to do and . . . we have a kind of gut feeling or professional judgement of what they need next.

Poppy's teacher also commented on the challenges of literacy teaching and learning and outlined the difficult decisions teachers need to make. She describes a tension in her school between the need to support children to achieve accuracy in the surface aspects of writing – such as spelling and punctuation – versus the importance of developing deeper aspects such as story composition:

> It's a real dilemma for us. Do we push them? Do we do things that we don't believe in, like sending spellings home all the time and forcing them to spell those things correctly? . . . I mean, the content of their writing is stunning compared to many, but it's just not held together right the way through. You know, they can't control narrative from start to finish, or they have got appalling spelling, or they have no punctuation, but it's got the makings of a great piece of composition.

Parveen and the *Party Games* lesson

Parveen and her classmates are sitting on the carpet facing their teacher. They start the lesson by chanting the lesson objective which the teacher has written on the board:

> *We are learning to write instructions*

The teacher asks the children to recall the previous day's literacy lesson, which had also focused on writing instructions. She asks:

Teacher: What made the instructions more interesting?
Child: Sequential language
Teacher: That's right

She elicits some specific examples of 'sequential language' from the children – these include 'first', 'next', 'after', 'after that' and 'now'.

The teacher produces a Big Book and asks who can read the title. There is lots of excitement and one child reads 'Party Games'. The teacher asks the children to name some party games, and they suggest 'hide and seek', 'musical chairs' and 'piggy in the middle'. The teacher gives an example of her own – going on treasure hunts with her sister.

The teacher opens the Big Book and the children read aloud some of the instructions that it contains. The teacher asks the children to identify some phonemes in what they have just read. One child suggests 'ite' as in 'items' and another suggests 'ou' as in 'found'; Parveen suggests 'or'. The children read out two further instructions and each time the teacher asks them to identify phonemes in what they have read.

For the next stage of the lesson the children are asked to sit quietly in a circle. The teacher switches on a radio tuned to a music channel, and produces a large wrapped parcel. There is general excitement as she tells them they are going to play 'pass the parcel'. She also tells them that afterwards they will be writing instructions for how to play this game. The parcel is passed around and one child eventually wins the prize it contains – some Easter eggs.

The children rearrange themselves so they are again sitting on the carpet facing the teacher. She writes *Pass the Parcel* on the board, and asks the children which instruction should come first. One child suggests 'get some friends to come round'. The teacher asks him to elaborate and he suggests 'then', which she praises as a 'good use of sequential language'. She writes his suggestion on the board and asks for some more. Another child offers 'when the music stops' but the suggestions are starting to dry up.

In the final part of the lesson the children are asked to write their own instructions for Pass the Parcel. The teacher rubs off the instructions she has written on the whiteboard and asks the children to work in their usual literacy groups. Parveen is in a group with three or four other high-achievers. The children write in their books until the bell goes for lunchtime.

Reflections on the *Party Games* lesson

One noticeable feature of this lesson is the explicit focus throughout on *language form* (as opposed to *language meaning*). The lesson starts, for example, with the children chanting out the lesson objective which the teacher has written on the board: 'We are learning to write instructions.' When the children are asked to recall key features from the previous lesson, she is particularly pleased when one child recalls 'sequential language', and reinforces another child's use of this kind of language later in the lesson. When the children read aloud instructions from the Big Book, the teacher again asks them to focus on language form – whether they can identify any phonemes – rather than on, say, the clarity or meaning of what they have just read.

Parveen's teacher pointed out that the current emphasis on language form, based on the National Literacy Strategy, is quite different from the one she herself experienced at school:

> I don't remember being taught any of what they are being taught now. We just sort of learnt it . . . I remember doing some bits with verbs and adjectives, but not as much as we do now, especially at this age. I think they do a lot more now

She also reflected on the impact that the Literacy Strategy has had on her teaching, noting both positive and negative effects:

> Sometimes I feel it [the literacy hour] restricts what the teacher can do in tasks because . . . we do seem to be sort of regimented. We've got to do this, that, and the other, and there isn't any other scope for imagination-type things . . . sometimes I find it quite hard to get it all in, in the hour. But . . . I can see why it's keeping everything fast so they don't get bored

These comments from Parveen's teacher support research findings that the National Literacy Strategy, with its emphasis on pace and speed, may not be conducive for cognitively rich interactions between teachers and pupils. English, Hargreaves and Hislam [📖 Reading 3.2] found that since the introduction of the NLS some teachers appeared to ask fewer challenging questions and had fewer sustained interactions with pupils.

One feature of the Party Games lesson is that the children actually play the game (Pass the Parcel) for which they subsequently write the instructions. Parveen's teacher explained later that this is something she was particularly pleased to have done:

> Yeah, it's been nice to see that when we've been able to do more practical activities and it's not just paper, pen and board activities that we have to do.. especially with the instructions, you know, if we play Pass the Parcel and made chocolate crunchies and made jellied oranges, which the children really enjoyed. I've always thought that doing a practical activity with the children gives them more consolidation of their learning – if they see it being done, they take it in more, or if they're doing it themselves. Providing that environment I think helps the children a great deal, and seeing that we've been able to do that's been good.

Geraint and the *My Home* lesson

The lesson starts with Geraint sitting on the carpet with the rest of his class. His teacher gets out a Big Book called *My Home* and places it on a stand at the front of the class. The children and teacher together read aloud from the book. The left-hand pages of the book follow a standard format in which various animals say, 'This is my home . . .', while the right-hand page describes in more detail the animal's habitat. The children, including Geraint, seem familiar with the book and read the left-hand pages with ease – they are much less fluent with the right-hand pages. The teacher ends this stage with the comment, 'Excellent reading' (unlike Seren and Luke, Geraint's school conducts all its lessons in English).

In the next stage of the lesson the children work in small groups. The children in Red Group each have a board in front of them with magnetic letters on. They use these letters to make the word 'snake', which is one of the animals in *My Home*. The teacher then gives each child a small booklet she has made based on *My Home*. The children read aloud in unison from their booklets.

The children in another group, Blue Group, each have a hand puppet representing an animal, as in *My Home*. They take it in turn to introduce themselves and say what they would miss if they didn't have their home. One girl, for example, says 'Hello, my name is Cow and I would miss my grass.'

Geraint is in a third group, Yellow Group. Each child in this group has a different reading book, and they read aloud individually from their own books.

In the next stage of the lesson the whole class is back on the carpet. The teacher is working with magnetic letters which stick to her whiteboard at the front of the class. She makes the word 'snake' and asks the children to say what the word is. She then covers the letters 'sn' and asks who can say what sound the remaining letters make. One boy, Neil, answers correctly. She then asks what sound the letters 'sn' make. The children are less sure and the teacher has to tell them.

The teacher then asks for volunteers to come to the front and make new words which end in 'ake'. Most of the children put their hands up enthusiastically. Geraint starts by putting his hand up, but then puts it down and puts his index finger across his lips in exaggerated style – this seems to be the class convention for 'I'm being quiet – so choose me!' Various children produce the words 'cake', fake', 'make', 'rake', 'bake' and 'flake'. When it is Geraint's turn he makes the word 'shake':

Teacher: What does that say?
Geraint: Shake
Teacher: Give them a shake then
          (Geraint wiggles his hips for the class)
Teacher: Well done!

In the final stage of the lesson, Geraint's teacher is working with Yellow Group. She uses a 'guided reading' approach which draws on the National Literacy Strategy's *Framework for Teaching*. Each child has a copy of the book *Jasmine's Duck*. The teacher asks them to read the title. Nia suggests 'James' but the teacher says it's a girl's name. Geraint suggests 'Jasmine' and the teacher says 'Good boy, Geraint'. The teacher and the children talk about the pictures of ducks on the front cover, and she asks Aled what sort of ducks they are. Aled hesitates and the teacher makes the initial sound 'm . . .' to help him. Aled suggests 'marigolds' but the teacher tells him they are 'mallards'. (It is perhaps worth noting that Aled has an extensive knowledge of dinosaur names.)

The children open their books, and the teacher suggests they talk about the pictures before they start reading. There is a lot of discussion about the characters in the story and what they might be doing and saying. Geraint is fully involved in the discussion. At one point he suggests Jasmine is saying 'I want that duck' and the teacher says 'That's a good idea, Geraint'. Later the teacher elicits from the children various possible endings to the story and writes these on a flipchart:

> *Kate took the duck home*
> *Kate took the duck to Jasmine*
> *Kate looked after the duck*

The children read aloud together a page from the book. The page contains the words 'ill' and 'I'll' and the teacher writes both these words on the flipchart. She explains how they are made from the same letters but have different meanings, and that this is due to the apostrophe (which she calls a 'flying comma') in 'I'll'.

Finally, the teacher asks the children to read the story quietly to themselves. At the end of the story it is revealed that the duck which Jasmine is concerned about is actually a toy duck. The teacher returns to the flipchart and puts an 'x' next to the first and third endings. She adds to the second ending '*but it wasn't real, it was just a toy*'.

Reflections on the *My Home* lesson

This lesson has many of the features we have already seen in the three other lessons. It is carefully planned and has a clear structure. The children work both at whole class level and in smaller groups, with the different activities designed to feed into each other. As with the other lessons, the whole class work is based around a Big Book – although here we see the Big Book augmented by individual booklets based on the Big Book, which the teacher has made for the children.

There are, however, some important differences between this lesson and the others. Here the focus is much more clearly on reading rather than writing. Indeed we see a range of different reading activities – these include the whole class reading aloud from the Big Book, a group of children reading aloud from the same books, and a group of children reading aloud from different books – as well as activities which analyse how words are made up from their component parts. Thus children get to experience, within a single lesson, a range of different ways of engaging with written texts.

The lesson also illustrates the use of the 'guided reading' technique. Here, Geraint's teacher guides the children through a detailed discussion of *Jasmine's Duck*, focusing on the pictures and how they might be interpreted, before asking them to read the text.

The children are thus 'primed' by the discussion for possible kinds of meanings and interpretations they might encounter in the text. Geraint's teacher was particularly enthusiastic about this technique, and felt that it represented a significant improvement on previous approaches:

> I think the whole thing of guided group reading has opened things like that up. I mean before when you just heard a child read you were so pushed for time and so desperate just to hear them read a few pages so they could change their book, you didn't have time for that, whereas now you're sort of looking through the book in the introduction.. and I mean like yesterday we were doing 'The Ghost in the Castle' and one of the children said 'Oh, I went to Cardiff Castle in the holidays', and then somebody else said 'Yeh, I've been there', and so they bounce off each other and it's just so natural you don't even have to plan it when you're doing guided group reading. It's the same with the Big Book, you know on the first day you're looking through the book, and talking about the pictures, and what they're doing is they're bringing their prior knowledge to their reading and that way they're going to be able to predict some of the words, like 'dungeon' . . . the boy probably in that group who is the least able at decoding, got 'dungeon' because he got it from the meaning because he'd been in a dungeon in the castle, and when you read you need to bring your prior experiences, your life experiences, to the books. I just think that, if you've got good guided reading sessions when the children are encouraged to interact with the pictures, at our level, then you know it actually provides them with a whole new strategy, and able to use the meaning cues.

Literacy learning at home and at school

We have now seen examples of Seren, Luke, Poppy, Parveen and Geraint involved in literacy activities at home and at school. We have also seen some of the children's comments on how they see the differences between reading and writing in the two locations. Box 3.1 reflects further on what these differences might be.

Box 3.1

Reflections on home and school literacy

Look back over the examples provided in Chapters 2 and 3 of the children's literacy activities at home and school. You might decide to focus on one or two children, or to consider them all.

What do you think are the key similarities and differences between literacy learning at home and at school?

You might want to think about some or all of the following questions:

- What is the purpose of the activity? Why is it taking place?
- Who is involved in the activity? What roles do they take?
- Who decides what happens? How much negotiation is involved?
- How is time being managed within the activity?
- What aspects of literacy are being used or acquired in each activity?

---

continued

- What kinds of texts are the children encountering in the two contexts?
- When the children are writing, who are the audiences for their writing? How far do they take account of the characteristics of their audiences?
- Do the children think they are learning about literacy? If not, what do they think they are doing?
- How – if at all – is the children's performance being assessed or monitored?

Parents and school literacy

Literacy learning in English and Welsh primary schools has changed dramatically over the last ten years. The National Literacy Strategy has transformed the way literacy is conceptualised, taught and assessed. For many parents, the methods their children are experiencing at school are very different from ones they themselves experienced in their own schooldays. Parents may be unaware of the changes that have taken place, or if they are aware of them, find them puzzling and confusing. They may lack confidence in helping their children at home, or worry that their children might be confused by different methods at home and school. (For a historical overview of reading teaching methods – some of which will have been experienced by parents – see ⌐ Reading 3.3].

Many of the parents we talked to couldn't remember much about learning to read or write. The main memory Seren's mum had of primary school related to building with blocks in the hall.

Int:	So how about your own experiences of learning to read, what was that like?
Seren's mum:	Er.. I don't remember
Int:	Can you remember any of the books that you would have been learning with or anything like that?
Seren's mum:	Was it Janet and John?
Int:	Yes, I was going to say with me it was Janet and John
Seren's mum:	Sorry, I can't remember. I can remember finishing off my maths really quickly one day and being allowed to go and play in the hall with the blocks, building blocks. That's all I can remember, I think. Dim and distant..

Other parents recalled worrying or upsetting occasions connected with reading. The mother of a boy in Poppy's class remembered

> I did learn to read fairly easily but I had one incident where a teacher made me cry when I was six because I had read the word 'the' on the previous page quite confidently and I was stumbling on this very same word only a few seconds later on a different page and I remember her being very frustrated and cross with me and making me cry because I couldn't do it.

whilst the mother of a girl in Geraint's class recollected:

> I was always below average at school. I think (that's) probably why I'm always a little bit paranoid and a bit anxious about the literacy, because I always remember I used to dread having to go up to stand with the teacher, because I remember going through.. you had to read words to them and you had to get to a certain level and I always used to be below my age at reading . . . I used to hate reading out at school.

Parents who did remember features of the way they learnt to read at school mentioned the following aspects

- 'flashcards' (where children learnt sets of words based on their visual appearance before reading them in a book)
- using colour coded books to progress in stages
- different approaches to phonics, for example not using signing or other mnemonics

Several remembered the Ladybird books, especially Peter and Jane. The mother of a boy in Parveen's class told us:

> Yeh, we used to do the Peter and Jane books and I used to take them home and my sister used to read them to me and I used to memorise them, so that's how they never picked up that I couldn't read . . . I'd look at the picture 'Jane has the ball', you'd sort of look and think – yeh, Jane has the ball. That's how I did it. But I got to 11 and I still couldn't read. But there you go, I can now.

One parent had bought these books to read with her children at home.

Parents were also vague when it came to talking about learning to write at school. A few remembered that mostly they wrote stories. Geraint's dad told us

> No, it was all from your own head. The learning to read was the ABC on the blackboard, which I knew already, and then you literally had to start out by writing your own short stories and then the teacher would come along and start pronunciating.. putting.. you know, pronunciating where you should have put pronunciations, putting capitals where they should have been, and so you got used to the {form of} language and putting full stops where they should be. And that's how we learnt.

Several remembered learning the mechanics of handwriting, like the mother of a boy in Poppy's class.

> I remember, um.. yeah, I do remember a couple of vague things, is having the sort of little A5 notebook which were all lined and I remember them being spaced out with three lines, so you could form your letter on those specific lines with the tails touching the bottom line and the long.. touching the top line, that sort of thing and I remember the teachers on the blackboards actually telling us which way to form each letter so they're all, you know.. you start at one point and you go through to the next.

The mother of a boy in Parveen's class compared the age at which she herself learnt 'joined-up' writing with her son's experience:

> I remember I didn't learn joined-up writing until I was about 9 or 10 or something, and now they're expected to do it straight away which I find quite difficult, I suppose. I don't really like teaching joined-up writing this young when they're only just learning to write, I do find that difficult, I think I wish they wouldn't do that, because it makes their writing look so scruffy when they're so young.

A few mentioned difficulties with spelling:

> I can remember probably about, perhaps Rhett's age, maybe a bit younger, I didn't know how to spell 'who'. That was my only memory, just the first time, and we

had to write a few sentences under a little picture. And I was just.. – how do you write 'who' phonetically. I just couldn't do it. I think I ended up writing HW or something like that, but that's all I can remember about reading and writing.

Some felt that their knowledge about language was limited. The father of a friend of Poppy's admitted:

And I still generally probably don't punctuate things, because I haven't a clue where to put them. Arden tells me about verbs and things and it doesn't really mean a great deal to me – I couldn't tell you what a verb was. I could probably tell you what a noun was, but that's about as far as it goes. And I use full stops and commas and that's about it. In fact, I rely on the computer very heavily now for spelling and, I guess, punctuation as well.

Box 3.2

Parents and school literacy

Reflect on the four literacy lessons we have described in this chapter. Think about other literacy lessons you have been involved with. Look at them from the perspective of parents whose own experiences of school literacy may go back 20 years or more.

What aspects of current school literacy might parents find surprising if they sat in on a literacy lesson today?

You might want to think about some or all of the following:

- the focus on 'literacy' rather than 'reading' or 'writing'
- the way in which lessons are planned and structured
- the emphasis on children working at whole class or group level
- the absence of teachers hearing individual children reading
- the use of resources such as Big Books as opposed to flashcards
- the use of technical terms to talk about language
- the pace of lessons.

Conclusions

This chapter has focused on literacy learning at school. We have looked at how Seren, Luke, Poppy, Parveen and Geraint experienced literacy lessons in their classrooms. We have reflected on the differences between home and school literacy learning, and on the ways in which current school literacy practices may be unfamiliar to parents today.

These reflections raise questions about whether and how parents can be made more familiar with school literacy practices. They also raise broader questions about whether and how home and school literacy can be brought more closely together. In the next two chapters we provide some practical answers to these questions.

Further reading

📖 *Reading 3.1*

Kathy Hall discusses the impact of recent government educational reforms in England, with a particular focus on primary literacy. In Chapter 4, 'Outstanding literacy teachers and their teaching: teachers not packages!', it is suggested that effective literacy teaching is characterised by features such as integrating various literacy modes so that children talk and write about what they have been reading, and read and write with and for their teacher.

Hall, K. (2004) *Literacy and Schooling: Towards renewal in primary education policy*, Aldershot: Ashgate Publishing Limited.

📖 *Reading 3.2*

The authors of this paper report research on teachers' perceptions of and responses to guidance in the National Literacy Strategy on the need for interactive teaching that is 'well paced with a sense of urgency'. It is suggested that although the NLS has increased the rate of pupil contributions, opportunities for extended interactions tend to be reduced.

English, E., Hargreaves, L. and Hislam, J. (2002) 'Pedagogical dilemmas in the National Literacy Strategy: primary teachers' perceptions, reflections and classroom behaviour', *Cambridge Journal of Education*, 32: 9–26.

📖 *Reading 3.3*

Anne-Marie Chartier provides an interesting history of the teaching of reading. Although it stops at the end of the nineteenth century, it describes many of the methods that would be used during the following century and which parents might have encountered during their time at school.

Chartier, A. (2004) 'Teaching reading: a historical approach', in T. Nunes and P. Bryant (eds) *Handbook of Children's Literacy*, Dordrecht: Kluwer.

Chapter 4

Literacy activities that take school to home

In this chapter and the next, we suggest some practical activities for linking home and school literacy learning – what we have called *home–school knowledge exchange activities*. These activities were developed and implemented by teachers at the schools attended by Poppy, Parveen, Luke, Seren and Geraint, with the support of the literacy teacher-researcher on the project team. We present the activities as examples which other practitioners can use as they wish – trying them out as described here, amending them to suit their own particular circumstances, or using them as starting points for developing their own ideas. Along with our suggestions about what to do and advice about practical considerations, we have included accounts of how things worked in practice on our project and what sorts of responses the activities received from different participants – this will enable readers to assess for themselves how the activities might be used, adapted or developed.

Knowledge can be exchanged in two directions – *school-to-home* and *home-to-school*. At present, most information which passes between teachers and parents goes from school to home – what Jackie Marsh (2003) has called 'one-way traffic'. Much of this information is in written form – such as newsletters, information sheets or invitations to events. In this chapter, we describe some more unusual methods for communicating in this school-to-home direction which rely less heavily on the written word. In Chapter 5 we describe activities where the flow of information is in the opposite direction, from home to school.

What do parents want to know about school literacy?

A first step in developing school-to-home activities is to find out what parents actually want to know. Clearly there is little point in sending home information which parents already have or which they will not find useful. A good starting point might be to review existing forms of school-to-home information and try to obtain feedback on whether they are providing what parents want. Often this can be done through informal conversations with parents at the beginning and end of the school day, or through asking parents when they come into school at parents' evenings or other events. Alternatively, a small number of parents might be asked to canvas the opinions of other parents and feed these back to the school.

Activity 4.1 Making a video of a literacy lesson

One of the most effective strategies for sharing information about school literacy learning with parents is to make a video of a literacy lesson and provide copies for each family. This approach has a number of advantages:

- a video allows individual schools and teachers to show parents how they specifically approach the teaching of reading and writing

What our parents wanted

We used questionnaires (translated into home languages where appropriate) and parent discussion groups to find out more about what our parents wanted. They made several suggestions for improving school-to-home communication in general. These included:

- regular (weekly, monthly) newsletters on topics/targets being covered in class
- more informal parent–teacher meetings
- set weekly times when teachers are available to see parents
- fun activities that can be taken home from school.

One important aspect to emerge was a desire to know more about how their children were being taught literacy, particularly in order to synchronise approaches between home and school. As one parent pointed out:

> It would be helpful to know the school's way of teaching [literacy], for consistency with your child at home.

Some parents also made a number of specific suggestions as to how this kind of information might be conveyed. These included:

- a chance to sit in on a literacy lesson
- teaching sessions for parents, to demonstrate methods used by the teacher
- more information and advice on how to help
- a home–school reading diary.

- a video provides parents with a window on what is happening in the classroom which might otherwise be difficult to arrange (e.g. if parents are working all day)
- making a video may be less disruptive than having groups of parents visiting a classroom
- a school-made video which features their own children holds more appeal for parents than a government-produced video about the National Literacy Strategy
- parents may prefer to access information visually rather than through reading.

Planning to make a literacy lesson video

A key issue to address is that of informed consent. While teachers do not need to obtain individual written permission from parents, they do need to inform parents in advance that their children will be filmed, and give both parents and children the right to opt out if they want to. Parents also need to be informed about plans for the finished video, for example who will receive copies and arrangements for screening.

The content of the video needs to be carefully planned by the teacher to decide what is to be filmed, why certain content will be included and how best to portray it. If practical, every child should feature in the video, and teachers also need to consider how far they will attempt to give equal time to individual children.

There are different ways the video can be shot and edited. Some teachers might prefer to have plenty of footage which can subsequently be edited down – and modern digital technology makes this a lot easier than it used to be. This approach gives more control over the content. Since the results will be made public, teachers may want to edit out some aspects – for example if a child is being represented in a particularly poor light. However, it may be simpler to plan the content and timings in detail in advance, so that no further editing work is needed. It's also useful to set up a camera in the classroom prior to filming, so that the children become used to it and to the whole idea of being filmed. If teaching assistants are not featured, they can be asked to operate the camera.

It may be desirable to provide extra information along with the lesson content. This additional material might draw attention to or highlight particular features, provide explanations as to why certain aspects are the way they are or suggest ways parents could build on or support what they are viewing. One way to provide such information is to arrange for screenings of the video for the parents, at which the teacher is present and able to provide context for the video and answer questions as they arise. Providing a number of such screenings at different times of the day and in the evening will maximise the number of parents who are able to attend.

An alternative way to include additional information is for the teacher to record inserts for the video. In these the teacher can explain what is going on and why things are happening in a particular way. Such inserts can be especially helpful where there are children in the class who have English as an additional language, as the inserts explaining what is happening in the lesson can also be recorded in home languages. Copies of the video with the lesson and the inserts can then be made for each child to take home to their family.

Making videos of literacy lessons – what we did

All of the schools in our study made a video. Two decided to focus on writing and two on reading. All the videos illustrated the structure and features of the literacy hour. One of the writing videos started with a whole class session where the teacher modelled writing a conversation between two characters based on the contributions of the children. The speech of each character was shown in a different colour, a technique shown in a Big Book used at the start of the session. As she was writing, the teacher made mistakes, e.g. spelling 'you' as y o o, which the children corrected as they noticed them. She explained her strategies in an insert spoken directly to the camera. The children were then shown working on a similar task in groups. This section was followed by a second insert where the teacher explained aspects of group working, such as which groups she worked with and why. The video also included an episode in which the teacher and an individual child set new personal writing targets together. Again the teacher explained in an insert why targets were set in this way.

It can be a little daunting to speak straight to a camera when producing the inserts. Teachers may find it more natural if someone asks them questions relevant to the lesson content which they then answer, speaking to the questioner rather than the camera. This format is often seen in local news broadcasts.

If the video has been recorded digitally, then copies can be made on disc. If schools find it too costly to make copies for each family, a cheaper alternative is to make four or five copies which parents can borrow and view on a rota basis. Videos can also be made in other curriculum areas such as mathematics, in order to build up a class or school collection of materials for parents. A third way to supplement the material appearing in the video is to produce a booklet that children take home along with the video.

Additional materials – what we did

Booklets were written to accompany each video. These reflected the ethos and aims of each school and provided an opportunity for teachers to illustrate certain strategies with parents for helping their children at home. For example, the following suggestion was included in one of the booklets for parents:

When your child is stuck on a word try saying:

- *look at the picture*
- *what would make sense?*
- *what sound does the word begin with?*

These booklets emphasised a partnership approach:

This pamphlet outlines some of the teaching strategies used in school and we hope that it will be useful to you to offer children consistent support at home . . . If you would like further information about supporting your child's writing, please come and discuss ideas with the Year 1 teachers. We would also love to share in the writing successes that children are having with you at home

A page from one school's booklet is reproduced in Figure 4.1.

Guided Group Reading

- Every child is a member of a reading group, with children of a similar ability. They will have one or two group sessions each week with the Teacher or Learning Support Assistants.

- Children are introduced to the new book by looking at the front cover and the pictures. This discussion work is important as the children are encouraged to predict what might happen, using their previous reading experiences.

 ❖ ***When your child brings home a new reading book, talk about the pictures together, before he/she reads it for the first time.***

- At ..... Primary the teachers like Guided Group reading sessions as they give an opportunity to teach reading skills. In the video the children have their first introduction to the apostrophe.

- The children then read from the new book independently, and the teacher listens to each child.

Shared Reading; The Big Book

- Each teacher chooses a new Big Book which the children read together every day for a week.

- The Big Book is a stimulus for most of the language work which the children do in class.

- There are a variety of Big Books including storybooks, poetry and information.

- The teacher models the reading, including expression, and the children have an opportunity to join in, gaining in reading confidence as they do so. This enables children to read at a higher level than they could manage individually.

 ❖ ***Have you tried sharing a book with your child, where you read most of the text and your child reads just a little?***

Figure 4.1 Extract from a booklet for parents

Our experience – what people said about the videos

Some parents commented that they felt more able to support their child's learning after viewing the video. In the following example, the mother of one of Geraint's friends explained how shared reading with her son had changed. Previously, they would start reading or decoding straight away, whereas after watching the video they would look through the book and talk about it first:

> I learnt a lot from that [watching the video] because I never used to read a story first, I'd just open the book and [he'd] start to read it, and that's where you get your 'no expression'. But if you've read the book and you look through the pictures and you explain the story, by the time you get to read it then you're more into it, aren't you, because you know what you're looking at. It makes sense, it does make sense, but you don't think to do it until you're actually shown yourself, do you? But it was, it was really interesting, that was. It sort of opened my eyes more to how they learn.

Another common parental comment was to express appreciation for being able to see how their child responded to teaching in the classroom. This was especially true for parents who for various reasons did not go into school:

> It's always good to see how it works in the classroom, because that's not an opportunity you'd normally have, is it, unless you were a helper.

One father who hadn't visited any lessons said:

> It's only a little snapshot of one, you know, one session, but I liked the way that Mrs X spoke to the kids and then asked them to.. it was very much kids' participation and involvement, you know, she made deliberate mistakes on the drawing board and they all kind of shouted out 'oh that's wrong' and stuff. But, yeah, and so it was quite nice to see, yeah, it was quite nice to see.

The videos had other, less expected outcomes. For example, many parents said that they felt more aware and appreciative of the teacher's role in the classroom. Seren's mum told us:

> There's a lot of coordination, isn't there, a lot of planning, getting it all sorted. It's amazing, and there just looks like such a lot of children, just hundreds! Yes, it's amazing.

Teachers commented that the activities had strengthened their relationships with parents and were very pleased with the video as a medium for sharing information:

> The video was most successful. It showed them five things, very easy, that they could do at home with their own children.

It also provided a starting point for schools to build on various aspects of their partnership with parents. One teacher noted that:

> The video was really good for bringing people in to find out about what we were doing.

Box 4.1

Making a video – things to consider

- What reasons might there be for making a video of classroom practice?
- What might be included and why?
- How should the children be represented in the video?
- What arrangements could be made for showing the video to parents?
- What could be arranged for parents who could not/did not attend screenings located in school?
- What supporting materials might be especially valuable?

Activity 4.2 Using out-of-school settings to share school achievements

In most schools, meetings and events that share and celebrate children's achievements (such as parents' evenings and class assemblies) are carried out on the school premises. This normally happens for practical reasons: schools and classrooms are generally welcoming and comfortable places where children's work is attractively displayed, and the setting is familiar to parents, children and teachers. In addition, this sharing usually happens at times which are decided by and convenient for the school. For many schools this means during or immediately after the school day.

For some parents, however, these times and places may not be convenient. In many families both parents work and many will have jobs where there is little flexibility for taking time off to visit school. In a number of cases one parent takes on responsibility for all school liaison. For some parents, their own experiences of school (in many cases very recent) can also make these visits problematic. For them school is not seen as a 'neutral' space, but a place that can evoke very powerful memories and feelings that may not be positive. Furthermore, many children spend time moving between childminders, nannies and other family members. These important figures in a child's life may remain unacknowledged by their school, and whilst many might not welcome formal partnership, some might appreciate opportunities to develop informal contacts with the school.

Schools can attempt to redress this imbalance by considering possible out-of-school locations for sharing and celebrating children's work. Some schools have obvious alternative locations such as community centres. For others it is more difficult, and care has to be taken that any chosen venue is suitable for all parents (which might, for instance, rule out pubs and clubs). It is also important that any signs and labels used in such alternative settings reflect the languages that are used by the wider community. In addition, parental permission will be needed for displaying photographs of children in a public place.

The supermarket activity – what we did

At Parveen's school, a supermarket was used as the location for a knowledge exchange exhibition of children's work. This school had been formed by a recent amalgamation of an infant and junior school. The parents acknowledged the benefits of the merger and welcomed

continued

the phasing out of mixed-age classes. They recognised that the newly built premises resulted in a school that was a more pleasant and well-equipped learning environment. Some parents, however, particularly those whose children were in the infant school, were apprehensive about the changes. They commented that the ethos of the school had changed since the amalgamation, and that it did not seem as welcoming. In response to this, an exhibition was set up in a local supermarket in order to share information with parents and the wider community about various activities that had taken place over a period of two years.

The supermarket exhibition was designed as a casual 'drop in' event located in a neutral environment that was accessible both to parents who would not necessarily feel comfortable coming into school and to those whose lifestyles precluded attendance at school-based events. In order to attract a wide audience the exhibition was open throughout the day, from early morning (before school started) to the evening.

There were many reasons why the supermarket was chosen to host the exhibition. It was opposite the school entrance and many parents used the car park when picking up and dropping off children. It was also used by a wide cross-section of the local community and was open for extensive periods. Before starting this activity permission was obtained from individual parents to display photographs of the children.

The exhibition itself contained a wealth of materials and information. There were books that children had written together with parents and siblings. A television and video were set up and the video that the teacher had made of the class literacy hour played on a continuous loop. Booklets containing *Guidelines for Reading* were available, as well as the booklets that accompanied the video. Individual and class photographs of the children working on other home–school knowledge exchange activities were displayed together with some of the written work they had produced. There was also information in a variety of formats, including free copies of DfES publications such as magazines for parents and videos about literacy in community languages.

Figure 4.2 The supermarket activity

The atmosphere was very different from a more conventional 'school-based' event and the neutral location proved to be an important factor in this. There were no set attendance times, and indeed no pressure or obligation to attend at all. Refreshments were offered to parents and children (they were invited to have a coffee in the supermarket café, paid for by the super-market). More importantly the event was open to friends, the wider family and community.

It was important to choose an effective strategy for informing parents about this exhibition. Children were invited orally at school so that they knew about the event and could give further information to parents and carers, and parents also received a written invitation. Care was taken to make sure this included all the relevant details and looked attractive. Teachers also invited parents personally whenever this was possible.

Our experience – what people said about the supermarket exhibition

The attendance at the exhibition was impressive, with over 60 per cent of the parents with children in the class visiting. Many came on more than one occasion and brought along friends and relations. It was interesting to note that quite a few fathers attended along with several older brothers and sisters. Parveen's mum, who had not previously participated in any school based events, visited with the children and on her own. Parveen's grandfather, aunt and cousins also visited.

The children seemed really proud to have their work displayed in such a public forum. As one mother pointed out:

> She felt chuffed, because some of her school friends came over and she was saying 'that's me there with my mum, here's my book'. And she was showing everyone her book and you know the picture.

Parents were pleased that the children's work was being displayed to a wider audience:

> It was really nice and I thought.. it got other people involved as well, really, outside of the school. They could see what the school was doing and how.

One activity which was part of the exhibition was a home–school knowledge exchange activity in which children take into school important objects from home (see Activity 5.1, page 53). The exhibition enabled the parents to see how the activity had been built on in school. One child had taken in a *Bagpuss* video which had been his mum's when she was little. When his mother was asked if she had seen the exhibition she said:

> Yeh, we did yeh, and saw what he'd written about the Bagpuss video – 'It was my mum's video and I took it in because I like it' . . . I think he was quite proud of seeing his work displayed because there was a picture of the Bagpuss he'd drawn. I think he was quite proud of that. I think it gives them a sense of pride in their work doesn't it . . . being displayed in a shop.

The children's teacher commented on the parents' increased interest in their children's learning, and felt that her own involvement in this activity had aided her continuing professional development – she had built up a portfolio of the materials produced and commented that she intended using these at future interviews.

Box 4.2

Using out-of-school settings – things to consider

- What out-of-school settings (clubs, community centres, libraries, etc.) might teachers use to share work with a wider audience?
- What would the purposes of such a sharing be?
- What materials/advice might teachers like to share with parents in such a setting?
- How might parents and other family members be involved in setting up such an activity?
- How might the event be publicised most effectively?
- What arrangements could be made for staffing events in out-of-school settings?

Activity 4.3 Developing the use of the reading diary

We saw in Chapter 3 that there have been dramatic changes in recent years in how literacy is taught in schools. Innovations such as the literacy hour, interactive whole class teaching, Big Books and guided reading are now standard practice throughout England and Wales. As a result, parents may feel that the teaching of reading is now very much the prerogative of the teacher. They may feel less knowledgeable about the methods used in school, and less confident about supporting their children's reading at home. Some parents we spoke to were worried that the approaches they used might be inconsistent with those adopted at school:

> It would be helpful to know more about strategies used for teaching so that help is relevant [and] doesn't confuse.

We also saw in Chapter 3 how the materials used by teachers have also changed. In many schools boxes of books from which children chose one to take home have been replaced by sets of guided readers which remain in school. The reading diary, which gave parents advice on how to support their child's reading and which accompanied these books home, has disappeared from many schools. These diaries provided guidance for parents and acted as a vehicle for parent–teacher dialogues between home and school. Although not all parents wrote in the diaries, many welcomed the opportunity to ask advice and bring matters to the attention of the teacher.

In Chapter 2 we referred to research previously carried out by some members of the project team into the support strategies used by teachers and parents when they read school books with children. In that project, we explored the extent to which parents and teachers used 'conversing'. This was talk that helped children to make sense of the text, make links between the text and children's experience and respond personally to the text. An important finding of that study was that teachers tended to use more conversing than parents. In a follow-up study (Greenhough and Hughes, 1999) we found that some parents were encouraged to use more conversing through the use of a home–school diary containing guidelines relating to this form of reading support, supplemented by conversing grids that the children and parents could use together. The design of the diary contents was devised to highlight reading practices that parents might not have considered, and foster their use.

A diary booklet – what we did

In one of the schools where the focus of the video had been on writing, communication about reading was developed the following year through the production of reading guidelines. The aim of the guidelines was to give parents ideas about how to help and support their child's reading, to encourage dialogue around the book, and to make reading more than a simple decoding exercise which could often become a chore.

An A5 booklet was designed, entitled *Help your child become a better reader*. The booklet contained two diary sections, one of which was concerned with the participants' emotional responses to the text. This section contained two grids, one for the child and one for the parent/carer, in which they were asked to record their responses to the book: e.g. *Today my book made me: laugh/ feel sad / feel worried, etc.* (see Photocopiable sheet 4.1). The use of the grids served to reduce the writing demand required for creating a record. The second section covered other features of conversing and asked parents and children to record aspects of their conversation when reading or sharing the book (see Photocopiable sheet 4.2). A new column was used for each reading occasion, and the child or carer could colour or make a mark in several cells, as appropriate, e.g. [Today we talked about . . .] 'the part I liked best', 'the part where the words were good' and the 'part where it was a bit like my life', following talk about those aspects.

Our experience – what people said about the diary booklet

Feedback from parents indicated that they valued this form of support. One parent with older children commented:

> I wish there had been that guidance when my child was in Year 2. I would have welcomed the support.

Another parent with younger children added:

> I hope the school carries on with this when my child is in Year 1 and 2

However, one parent found the grids rather constraining:

> I would rather simply talk to my child about a book she had read or I am reading with her, rather than asking set questions and filling out a grid. This may make it more relaxed – rather than seem like more 'work' at home.

This latter comment reminds us of the importance of monitoring the reception of innovations and getting feedback from parents. The grids were intended to free up reading sessions from simply being a decoding chore. However, if they themselves are seen as a chore by those who are already engaging in conversing, then they will be perceived as an unwelcome imposition of school ways on home practice.

PHOTOCOPIABLE SHEET 4.1

Today my book made me: **To be filled in by the child**

laugh					
feel sad					
feel worried					
feel upset					
feel disgusted					
feel excited					
feel cross					
feel happy					
feel frightened					
feel scared					
feel angry					
feel relieved					
feel something else					

Today my book made my helper: **To be filled in by parent/carer**

laugh					
feel sad					
feel worried					
feel upset					
feel disgusted					
feel excited					
feel cross					
feel happy					
feel frightened					
feel scared					
feel angry					
feel relieved					
feel something else					

Use a new column each time you read.
Think about the way the book made you feel when you were reading.
Choose the box or boxes that match up with the way you felt.
Make a mark in the box or boxes that match your feelings.
Any kind of mark or pattern will be OK.

PHOTOCOPIABLE SHEET 4.2

Make a mark next to the part you talked about today.
Use a new column each time you read.

Today we talked about:

the part I liked best									
the part I didn't like									
the part where the words were good									
the part that puzzled me									
the part where it was a bit like my life									
a different part									

Activity 4.4 Setting up a reading club

Setting up a parent/child club is a further means whereby teachers can communicate with families about aspects of the curriculum. A reading club can function as a forum in which parents' repertoires of book-related practices can be expanded. This can happen through informal chats, demonstration and modelling, and through embedding ideas in the additional materials provided for club activities.

There is already a long tradition of some parents coming into class to help with activities. However, as we have mentioned above, some parents may feel daunted by schools and classrooms. If parents can attend as a group with the support of friends, a club may be a more attractive proposition. Allowing children of different ages from different classes to join a club will increase the likelihood of parents having a friend who will also be attending. Providing refreshments can also help to promote a relaxed atmosphere. If parents' home language is not English, then it may be possible to make language support available in a club situation. You can read more about how this can work in practice in our companion volume *Improving Primary Mathematics: linking home and school.*

A reading club – what we did

In Geraint's school, part of a corridor was transformed into an area called 'The Bookworm Club', and this was brightly furnished with comfortable chairs, sofas and tables. One wall was lined with shelves on which books for children were displayed. Two copies of every book were provided so that adults and children could share the book with ease. Story Sacks that had previously been created by parents were also hung in the area. (Information about Story Sacks is available from the National Literacy Trust – http://www.literacytrust.org.uk/socialinclusion/earlyyears/storysackspractice.html and on the DfES standards site – http://www.standards.dfes.gov.uk/parentalinvolvement/pics/pics_storysacks/)

Figure 4.3 The Bookworm Club

The club was open every day before and after school. The invitation to attend included extended family members and some children came with a grandparent. Every Tuesday afternoon, a storytelling session was held in which teachers or other adults shared a story with children and parents, modelling this process. Parents were also given advice about additional ways of supporting reading with their child, e.g. relating the text to the child's real-life experiences. These messages were reinforced through pictures on the wall that featured a Miffy-like character, wearing the uniform of the school. There were also sheets that prompted children to record aspects they might have talked about such as what they liked (or disliked) about a book.

Our experience – what people said about the reading club

Like many parents, Geraint's mother had positive experiences of the Bookworm Club:

Mum: We sit down, have a book.. I'm allowed to have a cup of coffee as well, and he has a drink and a biscuit, and you read the book all the way through, and then you've got this chart, it's like a worm, and every book you've got.. there's 50 marks on the worm and after every book you've read you cross it off and then when you get to 25 you get a certificate, and when you get to 50 you get a certificate, and then when you get to 100 you get a certificate. And you get presents as well, little prizes as well . . .

Interviewer: So what do you feel about Bookworm, what do you think of it?

Mum: Well when I first heard about it I thought oh, that's going to be a load of {bitch}.. you know, like you do. But then when I started going because I started going with a friend of mine, with her daughter and Geraint, and they were getting on brilliant and I thought this is good, take half an hour out and have a cup of coffee and a chat with all the other mothers

Geraint also enjoyed going to the club. He had read a large number of books there.

Geraint: We go and read books and after we've read the book we colour in the worm in our bookworm book, and then the lady comes round with the tea, juice and biscuits and gives them to us, and then I choose one in the big sacks . . . there was The Hungry Caterpillar . . . there's fruits, and the caterpillar, there's a big board to stick all the fruit on, and then there's the book to read it with . . . I had the caterpillar and I just pushed it through the fruit

Conclusions

This chapter has described practical ways of sharing information about school literacy learning, both with parents and with a wider community audience. In the activities described there was a strong emphasis on ensuring that this information targeted parents' needs, and innovative methods such as video were used to involve as many parents as possible. We also found that it was possible to reach a wide audience by holding events in out-of-school venues such as a local supermarket.

We conclude with some questions that may promote further reflection on the exchange of knowledge about literacy learning in the school-to-home direction.

Box 4.3

Reflections on helping parents support their child's literacy

- How might teachers share individual children's targets with parents?
- How might teachers let parents know of any successes/breakthroughs that their children might be making?
- When literacy activities are sent home from school, what home literacy events might these be displacing?
- Is there a danger that activities sent home from school are carried out in ways which reinforce negative messages about literacy? How might this be prevented?
- How might teachers provide guidance and support for parents who do not speak English at home with their children?

Chapter 5

Literacy activities that bring home into school

In this chapter we continue looking at practical activities which link home and school literacy learning. Here, our focus is on activities that bring aspects of the home into school. As in Chapter 4, we present these activities as examples which other practitioners can use as they wish – either trying them out as described here, amending them to suit their own particular circumstances, or using them as starting points for thinking about new activities.

One area in which knowledge of the child in out-of-school settings is being seen as increasingly relevant is in the context of assessment. Traditionally, this inclination has been at its strongest in the Early Years. The potential contribution of parents is highlighted, for example, in the *Foundation Stage Profile Handbook* (QCA, 2003) where it is suggested that a more complete picture of the child can be created if parents' unique knowledge of aspects of their child's development is included in their profile. Sheila Wolfendale's (2004) discussion paper considers the possible extension of this perspective to all phases of schooling. Practitioners may wish to consider what types of information from parents they would find most useful.

What our teachers wanted to know and our parents wanted to share

We asked our Year 1 teachers what information they would like from parents. Below, we list some of the things the teachers said they would like to find out from parents about children's literacy learning at home:

- How much reading/writing do children do at home?
- How often do children choose to read, alone or with an adult?
- Do parents encourage children to read whilst outside the home, e.g. in shops, on posters, signposts, etc.?
- Are there any specific aspects of literacy where parents would like more support to help their child?
- Are there any areas that the child has expressed concern about?
- How confident are children in reading and writing at home?

The kind of information that teachers wanted from parents focused strongly on issues linked to the literacy curriculum. When we asked parents what information they would like to share with the school in order to help their child's literacy development, they tended to cite broader issues that related to their child's overall approach to learning, such as:

- information about their child's strengths and weaknesses so that the teacher can meet their individual needs

continued

- information about their child's out-of-school interests, including involvement in sports and membership of clubs (many parents felt their children were developing areas of expertise that the school did not know about or utilise)
- children's experiences of issues such as bullying and racism.

Although this last point referred to school experiences, it was felt that home was a place where children might be more likely to talk about their concerns, so that parents would have a perspective that was not necessarily available to teachers.

How might these kinds of information be shared? In some schools it might be possible to do this through informal conversations at the beginning and end of the school day. This is easier in some schools than others. Sustaining a teacher–parent dialogue is much more difficult when children are picked up from a busy playground or go home on a school bus. In contrast, when parents are able to collect their children directly from the classroom it is easier to maintain relaxed, two-way conversations.

Some of the information that teachers and parents want to share might not be forthcoming in informal conversations but would be better addressed at a dedicated meeting. Arranging and attending this sort of meeting can make demands on parents and teachers alike, and alternative methods for developing an exchange of information might suit some schools. For example, a brief questionnaire might be sent home at the beginning of each school year, which parents and children could fill in together. This might cover hobbies and interests, clubs attended, friends and family, the child's preferred school subjects and any other information that the family felt was important. The sample questionnaire in the *Foundation Stage Profile Handbook* has three sections in which parents are asked to comment. Each section is preceded by a pair of stimulus questions (see Figure 5.1).

(A) What sort of things does your child enjoy doing at home? Does s/he have any favourite toys, books or activities?

Comments:

(B) Does your child like to talk about things s/he enjoys at school – any special friends or activities? Is there anything s/he does not enjoy?

Comments:

(C) What else do you want to tell us about your child, including anything your child has done that has made you feel proud or happy? Do you have any concerns?

Comments:

Figure 5.1 Foundation Stage Profile – parent questionnaire

In some schools, setting aside an extra five minutes during a parents' evening might work better than sending home a written questionnaire.

However, knowledge-sharing in the home-to-school direction can involve more than the kinds of exchanges suggested above. It is important that home knowledge should be built upon and brought into the learning children do in school. In Chapter 2, we noted some of the varied ways children were developing understandings of literacy in their out-of-school encounters. It is desirable that knowledge exchange in the home-to-school direction should also try and find ways to bring children's own out-of-school knowledge into school. Inevitably this means that the children as well as the adults will be involved in linking the two worlds of home and school.

In the rest of this chapter, we describe activities we developed on our project. We start by looking at a simple device – the shoebox – where the flow of the activity is predominantly in a single direction from home to school. Later in the chapter we look at more complex activities where knowledge flows in both directions – home-to-school and school-to-home.

Activity 5.1   Using artefacts from home

In their research on motivating literacy learning in the nursery, Jackie Marsh and Philippa Thompson (2001) put together 'media boxes' with the help of parents. They were expanding the Story Sacks idea to include sets of items based on popular culture, such as Bob the Builder and Winnie the Pooh. The boxes were taken home and the parents and children talked about and played with the contents. It seemed to us that the idea could be built on to provide a vehicle for knowledge exchange in the home-to-school direction. However, in this case the boxes would be put together at home and brought into school to be used there. Since the intention was for children to bring in objects from outside of school that were significant to them, the collections were not just limited to popular culture items. As the idea was taken up and implemented, shoeboxes were given to the children as containers for their collections, so this became known as the shoebox activity. The schools developed their use in two distinct ways. One was to enable children to introduce themselves to a new teacher by filling the boxes with artefacts about themselves. The other was to provide inspiration for children's creative writing.

'All About Me' in a shoebox – what we did

In two schools the children used shoeboxes to introduce themselves to their new teachers. In Geraint's school, children took the empty shoeboxes home over the summer holidays, accompanied by a letter that explained the purpose of the box. Parents were asked to encourage their children to decorate the box and fill it with items such as photos, toys, postcards, a book or magazine, some writing or any pictures they had drawn, and anything else which might be 'special' to them. At the start of the new school year, the children returned clutching their decorated shoeboxes filled with personal artefacts.

Figure 5.2 is a photograph of Geraint's classmate, Courtney, with her shoebox and its contents. These included:

- a postcard from Courtney's cousin sent from Disneyland Paris
- glow earrings
- a guide to a caravan park

---

continued

Figure 5.2 Courtney and her shoebox

- Dad's drawing of Sleeping Beauty
- a train ticket, postcard and a piece of seaweed from Weston-Super-Mare
- a photograph of Weston-Super-Mare beach
- 'Art Attack' collage of a frog
- a piece of writing about going shopping and buying shoes, and going on holiday
- writing about family birthdays (helped by mum)
- writing about a party
- a *Cinderella* read-along tape.

The new teacher thanked the parents in a class letter at the start of the term.

> Thank you very much for the wonderful 'All About Me' boxes, we have enjoyed looking at them. I look forward to getting to know you and your child over the next few weeks.

The teacher also took part in this activity by filling her own box, giving the children information about her own 'out-of-school life'. She put in a key ring tennis racket and a pair of chopsticks (she played tennis and loved Chinese food), together with other personal items.

The teacher used the contents of the children's shoeboxes across the curriculum. In a mathematics lesson the items were weighed and measured. In a history lesson the children exchanged boxes and were asked, 'What can you tell about this person from the contents of their box?' However, it was in the literacy curriculum that the boxes really came into their own, with the teacher using the contents of her box as a model for the children. She built up a full week's literacy work around the shoebox contents – a copy of part of her planning is shown in Figure 5.3.

Day	Whole class work	Individual work	Plenary
1	Teacher to take out one item from own box. What does it tell people about you? Repeat with more items. Draw some of the items from the teacher's box in the centre of the word web sheet. Label the items in blue ink. Explain that they are nouns, they can be drawn/seen/touched.	Children draw and label nouns on personal word webs.	Children name nouns in the room.
2	Teacher to choose item from own box and describe using adjectives. Choose further objects and ask children to supply adjectives. Add adjectives in red ink to word web.	Children add adjectives in red ink to own personal word webs.	Teacher gives a noun, children choose appropriate adjectives.

Figure 5.3 Part of the teacher's literacy plan for the week, based on the shoebox activity

After the work had been carried out in the classroom the children presented an assembly around the shoeboxes, and parents were invited into school to watch this.

A previous literacy activity at this school involved the children keeping a scrapbook of summer holiday events. The children brought in mementoes from trips and visits they had made during the holidays. The response rate for the scrapbook had not been very high, however, and the shoebox activity was far more successful in engaging the children's interest, perhaps because its purpose had been carefully explained to them.

In Parveen's school, when the class teacher went on maternity leave, the children filled shoeboxes with 'All About Me' items in readiness for her replacement. The accompanying letter explained the rationale for this activity in the following terms:

We would like the children to make an 'All about Me Box'. They will be able to share their box with their new teacher after the Christmas holidays, and use the contents to write about themselves.

The children chose many personal items, such as baby clothes, photographs with grandparents (some of whom were deceased), and significant artefacts from their pasts such as books they had been given when they left nursery. One child even included a page from a newspaper

continued

featuring an article on childhood bereavement in which he was photographed. Parveen was helped by her mum to fill her box. She had:

- a small soft white toy dog called Fluffy
- a small squeaky frog called Dotty that her mum had given her on her birthday
- a timer (oil and water)
- a book, *Loudmouth Louis*, which came free with a box of cereal
- her special book called *You are Very Special*, presented to her at nursery
- photographs of herself as a baby taken by her dad.

Our experience – the 'All About Me' activity

Parents responded positively to the use of shoeboxes as an introduction to a new teacher, citing the enjoyment the children had experienced:

> That was really good fun . . . and it was really nice for the teacher because it gave her a chance to get to know the children a bit better . . . [It was] informal, so they could talk about themselves, a way to get to know the children. I thought that was really nice.

> He thought he was the bee's knees. He really enjoyed doing it . . .

> She was quite excited about it beforehand and she talked about it.

Several parents, like Parveen's, got involved in the activity themselves. One parent had helped her child by suggesting she include plastic animals, while others noted how the artefacts reflected their child's interests:

> Because he loves alligators and crocodiles, he loves watching them . . . So I knew to pick like the alligator . . . because obviously he knows quite a bit to talk about story-wise, to write about.

> He just put a favourite toy in, a favourite picture of him when he was a baby, and just stuff like that. His favourite food. I think he liked it, because it was all his stuff.

Parents also remarked on the confidence with which the children talked and wrote about their families and their interests:

> I think he enjoyed talking about things he knows. Obviously he's quite confident then to rattle off everything.

Parents appreciated the feedback they received from the teachers about how useful they had found the boxes, and when interviewed months later many could remember the activity in detail.

The teachers too were very positive about using the boxes as a way of getting to know their students. One commented that it had helped her learn more about individual children and their family circumstances:

> Because I didn't know very much about them . . . it helped me to get to know the children and their families . . . you know, if they had brothers and sisters . . . somebody brought

in some sporting awards that they had got from different activities, so yes it did broaden that knowledge.

Many children said that they felt the boxes helped teachers to have a more detailed picture of them as an individual. For example, Geraint was pleased that his teacher had seen a photograph of him and his dad outside Burger King:

> I think that she found out that me and my dad went to Burger King cos (in the photograph) we were outside Burger King meeting a soldier.

Using home artefacts to inspire writing – what we did

In Poppy's school the teacher recognised the potential for using children's home knowledge and interests to inspire their writing, especially creative writing. Her school had been considering strategies for improving children's writing, and she thought that using artefacts from home could have a considerable impact on this area. The teacher and children jointly composed a letter that accompanied the boxes home. Part of this letter is reproduced in Figure 5.4.

We are interested in finding out more about what motivates children to write, and also to produce high quality written pieces. The activities we have engaged in at school this term have, on the whole, been adult initiated ones, with the children inputting at a later stage.

The idea of the shoebox is for each child to be able to use it to collect items they think would be a good and motivational stimulus for writing. We have discussed together the sorts of things these might contain and these are some of the examples the children thought of:

> a special stone or crystal; rocks; shells; shiny pebbles; things from a beach; a 'magic' piece of paper or a book; photos; Christmas decorations or tree pieces; toys or teddies; rings or other jewellery; glitter; leaves; flowers; a star; drawings of imaginary things, places or people.

Figure 5.4 Extract from letter to parents about the shoebox activity

In the letter parents were also asked to discuss with their child what they wished to include. In order to off-set any misunderstandings or apprehensions at home about this activity, the teacher conducted a role-play session with the children, helping them to prepare a response if their parent asked, 'Oh no, what has that teacher asked you to do now?'

The children took home the boxes over the Christmas holidays and returned them at the beginning of the spring term. Over the course of a week all but three of the children returned their box. They took it in turns to present their contents to the class, explaining why they had chosen the artefacts and how they intended to use them in their writing. The children listed their box contents and planned in more detail how they were going to use them. Then they worked independently or collaboratively to produce texts. It was interesting to note that although there was no restriction on the type of writing that the children could produce, most chose fiction. When the draft was completed the work was word-processed, spiral bound and the author's photograph and details were added. The finished books were sent home together with a letter for parents (again jointly composed by the teacher and children) that outlined the range of

continued

writing that had been inspired by the boxes (see Figure 5.5). The letter also thanked parents for their support and asked them to suggest future activities.

> We made some great stories with the things in the boxes. Some of them were serials. Some stories were long and interesting. Some of us shared boxes and kept thinking of more things for the story, because we got more ideas. Some of us used other people's boxes to write about and it could be fun. Some of us found it easier because we had things there to write about. Some of us found it better because we didn't waste as much time thinking up ideas.

Figure 5.5 Extract from letter to parents about writing stimulated by shoeboxes

Our experience – using home artefacts to inspire writing

Poppy's teacher found that the activity was highly enjoyable for the children and that they were motivated and engaged. She also commented that the contents of the shoebox made a significant impact on the writing of many children, and that certain children made what she termed 'literacy breakthroughs'. Examples of these impacts are provided in Figure 5.6, while Figure 5.7 shows Nicholas' story.

Length

- Maisie's writing was great. She came up with a really extended piece compared to what she normally does.
- Certainly Jake came up with longer pieces than he normally does . . . he'll [often] say 'I'm really slow'. And he did work much faster on these occasions. [It] was great to see him and obviously he felt really good about that.

Organisation

- Arden finished a piece! Arden never ever gets an ending done! And she did finish a piece and she got that sense of satisfaction about 'I've finished. That's my ending. That's what it feels like to finish a story!' Because it never happens! Because she does the most stunning phrases, incredible story phrases, but you never get an end, not ever . . . And this time she did!
- Kyle really struggles with getting his ideas down. He has wonderful ideas in his head – can't ever organise them. And he did actually get a few sentences done. Which was lovely to see, in that you could see him sort of thinking 'Oh, that's great, I have got a bit more . . .' Because he can see other people covering pages.

Motivation

- Greg was very motivated . . . he often needs me to go over and get him restarted and he didn't need [this form of support] on that occasion.
- Toby developed an idea a lot more than he usually manages to do.

continued

Figure 5.6

Inspiration

- Poppy was another one . . . it really inspired her. You know, the ideas that she got from it were really good quality
- It worked well for Nicholas, definitely. I mean he came up with a really good piece. There was only one thing that he really wanted to write about and it was these jumping beans. But he had thought through a really good story about them, and he is one that would sometimes sit in a session and say, 'I just can't think what I'm going to write.'
- Miranda, she actually got really immersed in it and she did two really good pieces. Because she often gets a bit stuck what to write and it ends up a bit conversational almost. Whereas this time she'd really got some ideas for the plot . . . Because she's very able, the quality of some of her language is great, but she often just doesn't know what to do in the story.

Figure 5.6 The impact of the shoebox activity on children's writing

You know that the Jumping beans can jump as high as the moon, but now for there biggest challenge and that is to Jupiter. They made the wheel back into a wheel. (In their first adventure they first used it as a wheel and then they turned it into space suits). Just like last time they used a dice to start and to remember to leave the reindeer that they found in their last adventure.

(On the moon) They decided too have a picnic on Jupiter in a volcano. They went up and up in the air but they started well then got stuck just around the World. Wow! exclaimed the red Jumping bean we are stuck in the ring of air around the world. Lets do a really big bounce. So they did and then they landed on Jupiter. They saw erupting volcanoes everywhere, but it was very cold. 'We need some warm clothes' said the red Jumping Bean. 'Look! There's a wardrobe with clothes in.' 'Good' said the blue one 'Lets put them on'. There's a water bottle to put at the bottom of the food basket too keep our food warm. There must be something wrong
With my brain said the red Jumping bean
Because I thought it would be hot not cold!
Let's have our picnic now. We have got ,
Said the blue Jumping bean: Chips, bananas,
Apple's , Chicken ,Jelly Jumping beans and
Tubby Toast that they stole from the Telly-
Tubby's. Come on let's get it all out and eat it, said the red Jumping bean. Munch, munch ,munch went the Jumping beans.
Lets have our sweets now ,said the red
Jumping bean. No way! said the blue Jumping bean .But I've had 1 crumb and quarter of a chip ,said the red Jumping bean.
We haven't even had the chicken yet!
said the blue Jumping bean. While the blue jumping bean was still eating, the red jumping bean sneaked the basket and ate all the sweets. The blue jumping bean was full so he said he would eat his sweets when he got back to earth. They jumped down to England and the blue jumping bean opened the basket and his sweets were all gone! Greedy lump said the blue one to the red one.
The End.
By Nicholas.

Figure 5.7 Nicholas' story

Furthermore, the artefacts helped the children to share an area of interest or expertise with the whole class. Douglas, for example, placed photographs of his two pet budgerigars in his shoebox. Months later a fellow pupil could remember Douglas' presentation to the class in detail:

continued

He has two, one called Harry and one called Potter [laughs] . . . He said they're very funny. They fly on their side. And whenever Douglas says 'Come on', it goes the other way.

The teacher was impressed by Douglas' confidence during this presentation:

Because he's not one who does often contribute to the class discussions . . . although he's very bright and if you talk to him he's very interested in a lot of things, he doesn't have a high profile within the class . . . and I almost would have expected him to be a bit shyer, I suppose. But when he had things to talk about, that he cared passionately about . . . he did a very good presentation. There were other people too. That . . . shows they're actually more confident and outgoing in this situation than I'd expected.

Parents welcomed the children's enjoyment of the activity and were enthusiastic about the underlying ethos that valued children's out-of-school experiences.

[My child showed a] genuine sort of interest and enthusiasm. I mean, a lot to talk about, and . . . a very strong model that 'I am respected.'

Bringing artefacts into school allows home experiences, interests, thoughts and memories to gain a presence in school. The objects can be seen as embodying something of the children's out of school identities. It is important, then, that a sense of respect is established both for the items and what they represent. This may be established by initially sharing the contents of the boxes during Circle Times, when ground rules of respect are in operation. In Poppy's class, the activity was introduced after the teacher had been with the class for a term. The teacher preferred this timing since she felt that by then the children had settled in and felt more confident about revealing personal aspects of their out-of-school lives. However, we should recognise that where the shoeboxes were used by the children to introduce themselves to their new teacher at the start of the year, the activity seemed to work equally well.

One feature of the boxes that was noted by the teachers was the great diversity epitomised within them. Responding to such diversity is one of the challenges for the teacher seeking to build on knowledge exchange in the home-to-school direction.

Activity 5.2 Sharing books from home

Jackie Marsh (2003) observed that in the school where she carried out her research the range of texts available on the shelves did not reflect the range of texts read within the home. Favourites relating, for example, to television and 'Disney' stories were absent at school. However, as we saw earlier, when the children brought in their shoeboxes, there was a wide variety of texts amongst the artefacts. These included books in written form and as video and audio tapes. The shoebox, then, can work as a channel whereby texts owned by the children may be brought into school. In Chapter 2, we saw how children brought parts of texts together, appropriating and recontextualising different features in their own creations. This intertextuality was evident in the writing of some of the children in school where it operated to motivate and engage. One child, for example, borrowed a favourite phrase from a book in her box – 'Pass the gravy Sadie' – as the culmination of the Christmas story she was writing.

The next activity – a book sharing scheme – also encouraged children to bring in texts from home but this time as a stimulus to reading and finding information.

As with the shoebox activity, this activity recognised and enhanced the children's identities as experts in certain domains.

Sharing texts from home – what we did

Poppy's teacher devised the book sharing activity to complement work on non-fiction texts. Children and parents were invited to lend books or videos to support a geography topic about 'Animals from other lands'. Parents were informed that the items provided would be placed in a box in the classroom, and children would be able to borrow these for use at school and at home.

The parents and children responded very positively to this activity. Twenty-six books were brought in on the first day of the scheme and this had risen to sixty by the end of the week The texts were stored in a special set of shelves and were categorised by the kind of animals they were about. Parents came into the classroom at the beginning or end of the day to help their children choose an item to take home, and their choice was recorded in a filing system.

Our experience – sharing texts from home

Children were happy to lend their books. As one mother said:

> The whole thing about sharing as well, you know, he was quite happy to lend – and proud to lend his book. So I think it was a really good idea.

Several parents commented positively about how the activity had helped make connections between the children's home and school lives. One said:

> He was very keen to take in a book. Again, I think it's nice, this link. It's a physical link between home and school and knowing, you know, that book belongs to your home and you're sharing it with your school and your class. And I think all the kids responded to that and the thought of 'are you taking my video home or are you taking my book home?' you know. I think they quite liked that. Often the kids bring in something that they're very familiar with and it's very new and exciting for the other kids and so there's a sense of pride isn't there? I think that worked really well.

It was clear that the children handled the books and videos with particular care. They recognised that the children who brought them in might be quite attached to them, as the following conversation with Poppy shows:

Int: And what did people think about bringing their own books into school and letting other people share them, were they worried?

Poppy: Well, R [names girl in class], which I borrowed her book, the kitten one, she said be careful cos it's really old, so I thought like they were like precious

Int: Mmm

Poppy: So I think most people thought they were precious

This conversation is also indicative of further connections that were made through the activity. Several children took the opportunity to choose books that furthered interests that originated at home. Poppy, for example, had a cat at home that she was very fond of and her choice to borrow a book about kittens reflects this interest. She also knew who the original owner of the

continued

book was so the activity provided an opportunity for children to become aware of interests they had in common with other children. Another child noticed that a classmate was particularly knowledgeable about human biology: 'He likes bodies, he always had books about bodies.' This common interest also led to the children, especially the boys, reading the books together collectively in the mornings before school.

Some children developed their own activities around the books. Douglas, the owner of Harry and Potter, wrote a review of the video he borrowed about *Animal Pets* (see Figure 5.8).

***Animal Pets* video**

It shows you what animals you can have as pets. They have cartoon animals and real animals to make it good. I liked the dog Bits Because it didn't Show you gust one tipe of dogs But small ones to the bigest dog's in the world

---

Figure 5.8 Video review

One boy was compiling his own list of facts about animals entitled 'Did you know . . .?' Another child devised a quiz game for his family at home, whereby he made the noise of the animal and they had to guess what it was.

Duality – exchanging knowledge in two directions

Although the emphasis of the book-sharing activity was on knowledge exchange in the home-to-school direction, the teacher took the opportunity offered by this activity to also exchange knowledge in the school-to-home direction. In the letter sent home explaining the scheme, she also informed parents about the ways used at school to locate information in non-fiction texts (see Figure 5.9).

We encourage children to read the contents page first, to see if any of the titles appear linked to their question or area of interest. They are also pointed to the index to see if this contains the key words they are after, or any related words, which might help. We teach them that information books often have an introduction and that these are not always signposted very well, but may give them valuable information and save them fruitless searching. Once they have located a particular page we encourage them to look at headings to find the relevant section, not just to read the whole page from start to finish. We also encourage them to look for key words.

Figure 5.9 Extract from letter for parents about book-sharing activity

In the shoebox activity, there was also an element of school-to-home knowledge exchange. The teachers informed the parents about how their children's shoeboxes were used in school, and in one case the parents were invited into school to watch the children talking about their shoeboxes at school assembly. These exchanges allowed parents to become more aware of the schools' ways of doing things.

These activities enable both parties to become better informed about what is happening in the 'other' place. We use the term *duality* to refer to activities which involve the exchange of knowledge in both directions. In the rest of the chapter we look at two more activities where there was a sense of duality, involving both home-to-school and school-to-home knowledge exchange.

Activity 5.3 Taking out-of-school photographs

Photographs are a wonderful medium for sharing information. They can provide a richness and immediacy which children might find hard to record in other ways. They can also be seen as a way of conveying the intimacy of the home in the school setting. Parents and children, not the teacher, can be seen as the 'experts' on the photographs. In addition, the novelty of children being given their own camera to use at home can help to ensure a high participation rate.

Taking out-of-school photographs – what we did

We provided the children with disposable cameras at the start of a holiday period as this would enable them to use the cameras in a wide variety of situations. In each school the activity was linked to the curriculum, with children being asked to take photographs relating to their class topic – making a model vehicle, living things (including people), plants and growth, and the local environment. They were also asked to take photographs of things, places and people that were important to them. Figure 5.10 shows an example of a letter that was sent out to parents describing the purposes of the activity and asking for their support.

Dear Parent/Carers,

This term the children in Miss X's class are doing a topic about 'The local environment'. As you may be aware we are conducting research into links between schools and parents. We would be very grateful if you could help your child to take some photographs related to this topic using the disposable camera provided. (Development costs will be met by the project.)

The children have been learning about:

- their house and garden
- other houses nearby
- local landmarks. e.g. shops and churches
- pictures of living things, e.g. families, plants, animals and insects.

All these photographs will provide the basis for further work in school and at home over the coming term. This might include book making, writing activities, and making displays for the classroom. We would also be interested in any other activities that you may be involved in over the half term holiday (trips, visits, etc.) so photographs of these would be most welcome.

The cameras must be returned to school by Thursday 13th June for developing

It would be helpful, at a future date, to discuss this activity with parents. If you can help please sign at the bottom of this sheet.

Thank you in advance for your cooperation

Figure 5.10 Letter to parents about the photograph activity

Our experience – taking out-of-school photographs

In all four schools the children and their parents responded enthusiastically to the disposable camera activity and the participation rate was excellent. Many parents joined in the activity themselves, including Geraint's mother:

> We were actually doing it together . . . we were out down the road, took some photographs of the post-office, and then we came up here to the.. a few photographs of the bridge, and the Littlewoods building, and he thought it was exciting until the end of the roll came and he said 'I can't take no more pictures', I said 'it's gone', he said 'well get the camera then', he wanted our camera, I said 'well no because this is already'.. the camera that they had from the school was already paid for, the process fee was already included, so you didn't have to pay for post, and I said on mine you would have had £5 . . . But he was telling (the teacher) the next day what he took, what pictures he took, and then.. she was telling me all this, he took this one, he took that one, he did this and that and the other. And he was writing down what he took for his own purpose, he didn't take that to school, he kept that for himself, so that he knew what.. which.. he took.

At Luke's school, the children were asked to make models at home relating to their topic on transport and to take photographs of the process. As Luke's mum described, the use of the camera seemed to add to the enjoyment of the activity:

> Well, he really loved doing that, he made a rocket . . . and he was just pleased as punch with the photos . . . I think it's the first time I've seen him do something from start to finish without having any kind of.. any tantrums or.. there's Rhian nodding in agreement, he just completed it . . . he revelled in it. I think perhaps the camera as well, the fact that he was showing off the different stages . . . and knowing that all the other children had one as well and they would be comparing photographs, and it also added to it.. the sense of occasion.

The teachers were also enthusiastic about the children's photographs. One teacher who had linked the activity into a topic on 'Living things' commented that it was a 'wonderful way to kick-start a project'. In Geraint's school the activity was so successful that it was added to the language scheme of work under the topic 'Houses and homes'. Children working on this topic in subsequent years used a camera to record information from their homes and brought these photographs into school.

Providing an individual disposable camera for each child is clearly an expensive option. However, as the teachers pointed out, there are ways to adapt the activity to make it more affordable. For example, instead of every child being given their own camera a small number could be purchased for the class. The teacher could then organise the activity so that children shared the cameras and took turns to take three or four pictures each. Another option would be to use digital cameras on a rota basis – pictures could be downloaded on the class computer and would provide a valuable resource for future work. In addition, parents and children are increasingly likely to have mobile phones with cameras, and so photographs can easily be taken out-of-school and subsequently downloaded in school.

Photographs taken at home can be used in many different ways to support literacy learning. In two of our schools, once the photos had been developed, the children took them home to use with their families there (see next section). In the other two schools, family members were invited into the classroom to work with the children on their photographs.

Developing writing based on the photograph activity – what we did and our experience

Involving parents at home

In Luke and Seren's class, the children took their photographs back home, together with an album made from card entitled 'Ffotograffau/Photographs'. Parents and children were asked to select four photographs to stick in the album and write captions describing what was happening in them. The teacher was concerned that some parents might find it difficult to provide support for writing the captions in Welsh since most parents were not (natural) Welsh speakers. The pages of the album were therefore structured so that there was space for captions in Welsh and English, and the children and parents could choose which language was used. The teacher also offered to translate phrases, if required. Almost a third of the albums were captioned by the child either in Welsh or in Welsh and English. Just over a quarter were captioned by the child in English only. The rest were captioned by parents – half in English and half in Welsh or in both languages. More than two-thirds of those captioned in Welsh were from families where English was the home language. Once captioned, the albums were returned to school to be used there.

In Poppy's class, the children took home several sheets of brightly coloured mounting card along with the photographs. Again they were asked to select four photographs to stick on the card and write captions describing what was happening in them. All but three sets were captioned by the children – one set was captioned by the parent and the child, one set by the parent and in one set, the captions were printed on a computer. The captioned photos were returned to school and used to make an eye-catching display in the school corridor. An example of one child's captioning can be seen in Figure 5.11

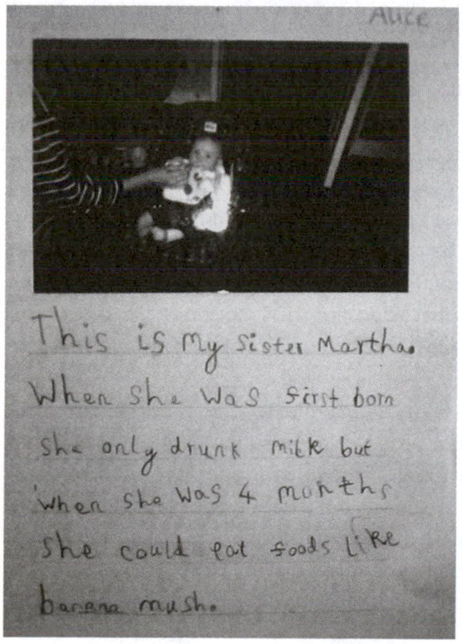

Figure 5.11 Writing inspired by the photograph activity

One boy in this class used the camera to take photographs of birds hatching in a nest. His parents described how involved he became in this activity and how it generated some excellent writing at home:

Mum: Oh that was great, that worked for us brilliantly because..

Dad: We were lucky weren't we

Mum: You can see it beyond the gate, that's clematis and there was a nest in there so they could climb up the gate and look right into the nest. I mean the photos that came out of it weren't brilliant but obviously we then looked it up and now they know what a female blackbird looks like, they can distinguish male and female, they know how long the eggs are there and it just lasted the whole holidays, it lasted the camera and then the day that he went to school.. the next.. for the.. to begin the new term, the babies had flown the nest, they'd been taught how to fly in the garden and it was just fantastic, he loved that

Dad: It was just perfectly timed because when we got the camera the eggs were in the nest and when we gave the camera back they'd flown the nest

Mum: The nest was empty. And I mean he didn't, it was something he resisted having because it's quite a formal thing to stick the photograph on and then we drew lines on for him to write, and 'no oh no, I don't feel in the mood' and I didn't want to push it and 'well we'll do it.. maybe see how you feel tomorrow'. 'Shall we do it?', 'no', I said 'it has to be done' and so it was a bit of an issue but once he sat down he actually really enjoyed doing it and to be honest I think.. I don't know if it's because I was looking over him, he produced, you know the best piece of work he had done yet I think . . . he wrote his neatest writing, I haven't seen such neat writing

The activity was very popular. One teacher commented that the children were really excited to get their photographs back and really proud of the work they brought in.

Involving parents (and siblings) at school

In the classes of Parveen and Geraint, the photographs were used as the basis for writing workshops in school. These workshops involved children and their parents working together, and were designed so that the parents were directly responsible for supporting their child's learning. As parents held a great deal of information about the photographs (taken in the out-of-school settings) their knowledge and expertise was invaluable. Figure 5.12 shows a letter inviting parents to the workshops: this was reinforced by a personal oral invitation where the teacher felt this would increase the participation rate.

During the workshop sessions the children made their photographs into books. Each day, the class teacher modelled the aspect they would be covering, by using photographs taken in school to make a large class book. On one occasion the children were provided with bubbles to stick around their photograph, in which they wrote questions for the reader to ask about their pictures. On another occasion they worked with the phrases – What is happening? What has happened? What is going to happen?

Although the response rate from parents was excellent, the teachers also invited the children's older siblings to the writing workshops in order to increase the number of children with a family helper. This was approached with slight misgivings in one school as some of these siblings would not have been an automatic choice (on the teacher's part) as positive role models. However, the impact that the activity had on these older pupils was noteworthy: they behaved in an exemplary fashion and supported other children as well as their own siblings. Their class teachers subsequently reported an increase in the helpers' self-esteem, behaviour and literacy skills. The school was so pleased by this additional outcome that this mentoring process was carried on after the activity had finished.

The teacher in this school also felt that the activity helped to build up good informal relationships with parents. She commented that the process of sharing and using these intimate photographs resulted in more personal contacts with families: 'I've got a better bond with the parents, they treat me more as a friend than a teacher.' Rather surprisingly, the teacher also reported that punctuality at the start of the day had improved after the activity.

The children felt that the activity had been exciting and enjoyable, especially when the results were displayed at a local supermarket (Activity 4.2). They also felt that the activity had allowed teachers to learn more about them, and they responded positively to the presence of their parents in the classroom. When asked about his father coming to help him in class, one child said that this was:

> Fun . . . he helped me. He reminded me what I could write and what things were and when they were

He also commented that his father had learnt 'how good I was at doing stuff like that'.

WRITING WEEK

Monday 18th–Thursday 21st November

Welcome again to the Home–School Project.

In Year 1, over the summer half term, you and your child used disposable cameras. The topic was 'Plants', and we also asked the children to take photographs of other things that interested them. Thank you for taking part in this activity. We would now like to use these photographs to make books, and we would like you to take part in this activity with your child.

You are invited to come into class to work with your child, on any morning from 8.45 to 10.00am.

We hope you can come.

Thank you

- -

I would like to attend the Writing Week.

My preferred day is:

Monday ❑   Tuesday ❑   Wednesday ❑   Thursday ❑

Figure 5.12 Invitation to parents to help their child's writing at school

For parents a key attraction of this activity is that they rather than teachers hold the 'knowledge' about the photographs, as the images represent aspects of the child's out-of-school life. However, it is important to recognise that some parents can still feel uneasy about being invited into the classroom to help with writing. Parveen's mum commented that she had felt rather diffident: 'A bit shy and scared a little bit. Too much children.'

It is important to recognise that some parents lack confidence in their own literacy skills. A way forward in using photographs from home might be to provide a range of activities, with some focusing on literacy whilst others might link to other curriculum areas such as art (e.g. making photograph frames), I.T. (making a slide show) or oracy (recording a commentary on the photographs). Ideas about how to use photographs of out-of-school mathematics can be found in our companion volume: *Improving Primary Mathematics: linking home and school.*

Activity 5.4 A trip to Cardiff Castle

Schools use class trips and visits as an essential part of the curriculum. In most cases these trips reflect current topics or curriculum interests. Parents are sometimes invited along as 'helpers' on the day but normally do not have any input into the planning or the follow-up.

Extending parent involvement in trips – what we did

At Geraint's school the teacher decided to involve parents more closely in a class trip. Previously this school had preferred to rely on teaching assistants rather than parents for help with trips. However, the photograph activity had revealed that parents had considerable knowledge about their local area, so a trip with parents accompanying their children was designed to build on this type of parental expertise. A visit was planned to a local landmark – Cardiff Castle – which most parents would have visited or had knowledge about. The intention was that, by recognising the parents' expertise, important knowledge could be exchanged between home and school both about the subject matter and about children's interests and learning approaches.

The activity comprised three parts: a pre-visit writing workshop, the actual visit, and a follow-up writing workshop. School staff felt that it was important to emphasise to families that all three elements were independent and that parents did not have to commit to all three. In planning any similar activity it is important to build in flexibility as many parents have childcare or job commitments and might be unable to join in all parts of an activity. You must also refer to your school's Health and Safety Policy when arranging any off-site visits.

The pre-visit writing workshop

To prepare for the visit to Cardiff Castle, parents were invited to school over the course of a week on the morning that their child's group was undertaking a writing task as part of their literacy hour work. This meant that for the class teacher there was no extra planning involved and parents could be easily accommodated in the classroom. During these sessions the forthcoming visit to Cardiff Castle was discussed and parents were asked to talk to their children beforehand to find out which topics or aspects were of particular interest to them. The teacher followed the conventional structure of the literacy hour, and parents supported their child in the small group session.

The day of the visit

The teacher used a number of carefully planned strategies to ensure that the level of parental involvement in the visit to Cardiff Castle was high. These were:

• All parents were invited to accompany the class by letter and by personal oral invitation where possible.

Figure 5.13 Courtney and her mother at the pre-visit workshop

- No charge was made for parents.
- Parents were encouraged to accompany their child on the visit even if they had not attended the pre-visit workshop.
- Parents were free to devise their own itinerary if desired, focusing on their child's interests.

Altogether around half the children in the class had one of their parents (mostly mothers) with them on the trip. At the castle itself, the children and adults were divided into two groups. Each group took it in turns to go on a guided tour of the castle itself and to explore the grounds. The grounds contained a keep, a Roman Wall and two military museums (see Figure 5.14).

The post-visit writing workshop

To maximise participation in the post-visit workshop, parents were given a choice of two days when they could come in to school, and were reminded that they could come even if they had not attended the previous events. One child's uncle attended this session as the child's mother could not attend. Materials relating to the castle, such as guide books and postcards, were supplied to support those who had not been able to join the visit.

During the workshop, the parents and children collaborated together to produce a story called 'My Castle Adventure'. A story board with six spaces was provided to help with the planning of the story. The teacher also produced a prompt sheet to structure the parents' support for the story writing. It gave examples of questions they could ask concerning the setting, the characters and the plot and included the following:

continued

Figure 5.14 The class at Cardiff Castle

- In which part of Cardiff Castle does the adventure begin?
- Who are the main characters in the story?
- What do they look like?
- How old are they?
- What happens in the middle of the story?
- Where do you go in the castle?
- Who or what do you meet?
- How does your adventure end?

Our experience – extending parent's involvement in trips

Parents enjoyed the opportunity to go on a visit with their children. Although Cardiff Castle was near the school and had been visited by many of the parents, most had toured the grounds rather than the building itself (perhaps due to economic constraints). One parent who went on the trip commented that:

> Cardiff Castle was lovely. I hadn't been into the castle myself, so it was nice. I've been into the grounds many times, but never on a tour of the rooms.

Parents also welcomed the chance to share in this part of their child's education: 'It made you feel like you were involved in something.' It was noteworthy that parents had made considerable efforts to accompany their child on this trip. One mother commented:

She [child] wanted one of us to go and I phoned him [child's father]. I explained I couldn't because of the baby, and I asked him.

She added that she felt her child had undoubtedly benefited from her father's presence: 'it's like doing something as a family as well isn't it?'

Several parents commented on how much they had gained from taking part in the workshops. Damien's mother made the following observations about the pre-visit session:

Yes, a lot.. I learnt a lot about him.. well, not a lot about him, but about the way you could make up stories, that was really good. (Damien comes into the room at this point.) Remember when we done down in the jungle with all the animals and you had to guess the animals? And they did role-play as well in the classroom, they had to pretend they were the.. oh, what's the.. the explorer, pretend they were the explorer and then put their goggles on and pretend they were going to see this animal, this type of animal in the book, and they had to guess which animal it was. It was just loads of different things they done with it, it was really good, really interesting.

Parents felt that the post-visit writing workshops had also been beneficial. The supportive nature of the sessions was also mentioned: 'the way they structured it . . . those sentences on the board, they were there to help you constantly'. And when asked if the activity had influenced how they would help their child with learning, one parent commented:

Yes, I've learnt more how to approach them . . . And with their doing stories and things like that . . . going into class has helped me, I've got more patience to sit there and do things.

As with the previous activity some parents commented that going into class could cause apprehension:

It is quite daunting, going into the classroom and you're thinking, 'Oh my God, what have I got to do?' But it's nothing major . . . it's just being there, and helping them and guiding them through what they've got to do. Because obviously there's not enough pairs of hands in the class anyway and the more you can help the better.

The children seemed to understand that during the writing workshops and the visit parents had an equal teaching role. One child was very appreciative of the help her mother provided: 'She helped me spell the words out, because I had really hard words to do.'

The teacher enjoyed the visit herself, saying, 'we had great fun!' She also felt that she had benefited from having the parents accompany them:

Yes, I think you get to, obviously, know the parents more and maybe understand the child more

The teacher noted that after the visit, many of the children's parents offered further support by bringing library books and other artefacts in to school (such as crowns that had been made at home). A Big Book of the trip was made to commemorate the parents' participation, and children and parents received their own smaller copies.

Conclusions

This chapter has described knowledge exchange activities which involve a flow of information from home to school. The success of these activities is indicated by the high participation rates and by the positive responses of the children, parents and teachers. The teachers valued the insights they gained into children's out-of-school worlds. Some of this new knowledge – for example the breakthroughs made by some of the children when their writing was inspired by the contents of their shoeboxes – impacted directly on the curriculum. In other cases the activities revealed more personal insights, and parents and children enthusiastically took up the opportunity to share these with schools.

Box 5.1

Reflections on home-to-school knowledge exchange

- How might teachers learn more about the out-of-school lives of the children in their class?
- How can this knowledge be used to enhance teaching and learning in the classroom?
- What areas of the curriculum might benefit most from this kind of approach?
- How can teachers provide opportunities for children to learn more about the out-of-school interests of their peers?
- How can teachers respond to the diversity of children's out-of-school lives?
- Do children have the right to keep their out-of-school lives private?

Chapter 6

Home–school knowledge exchange – benefits and challenges

This book is about home and school literacy, and how these can be brought closer together by what we have termed *home–school knowledge exchange*. In this final chapter we focus more closely on the central idea of home–school knowledge exchange. We say what we mean by this term, what its underlying principles are, and how they can be put into practice. We also look at some of the challenges faced by teachers and other practitioners who want to put home–school knowledge exchange into practice, and we spell out the benefits that might accrue if they do so.

What is home–school knowledge exchange?

Although parents and teachers know much about different aspects of children's learning, their knowledge tends not to be well-shared or built on. A central theme of this book is that we need to bring home and school together more effectively, enabling parents and teachers to recognise what each has to offer. Parents have a deep and intimate knowledge about their children – how they approach learning, what motivates them, what they know and what they want to find out. Similarly, teachers have a wealth of knowledge about children's learning at school and how to teach the range of subjects that comprises today's curriculum. But although teachers know much about the curriculum and teaching approaches, they may not know much about children's out-of-school worlds. And although parents know a great deal about children's home interests, their skills and their passions, they may know little about the literacy curriculum and how it is taught in school.

The Home School Knowledge Exchange Project was inspired by the idea that it would be beneficial for parents and teachers to pool their 'funds of knowledge' about children. We set out to devise activities that would result in parents' and teachers' knowledge becoming more explicit so that it could be communicated and shared in order to enhance children's literacy learning. Many of the activities described in this book have achieved this goal, showing that teachers and parents can indeed develop rich insights into children's literacy learning, and that home and school knowledge can be gainfully shared.

However, this isn't the whole story. When we started asking who was in possession of knowledge that informed literacy learning, we began to realise that often the answer was the children themselves. For example, when we examined children's stories, it was apparent that the range of influences children draw on at home when writing fiction is immense – books, comics, videos, DVDs, television and films. We saw in Chapter 2 how popular culture plays a pivotal role in this creative process: it provides an exciting stimulus for children's writing, and children draw on it for a multitude of ideas and themes. So we came to understand that when we think of knowledge being exchanged between homes and schools, this exchange is not just between parents and teachers, it also directly involves children's knowledge.

Together with our realisation that children's knowledge is highly significant was our awareness that it doesn't necessarily need to be parents who mediate the exchange of knowledge with teachers. At times children themselves provided very effective channels or means of communication. This was manifest with the shoebox activity (Activity 5.1), when artefacts were brought into school to support literacy learning in the classroom. It was generally the children who made decisions about what to bring and what to leave out. The significance of the chosen objects was highly personal and children were often encouraged by their parents to make individual choices. This resulted in children becoming the vehicles for home–school knowledge exchange.

At this point we can identify key principles that underpin the process of exchanging knowledge between homes and schools to help children learn:

- All families – including children themselves – possess important 'funds of knowledge' which can be drawn on to enhance children's learning in school.
- Communication needs to take place in two directions, from home to school as well as from school to home.
- One size does *not* fit all – home–school knowledge exchange cannot be imposed in a uniform way. Some excellent ideas that have been tried and tested in one context may not work in other settings, so be prepared to amend and adapt the ideas in this book.
- Treat diversity amongst children and families as an opportunity and not a problem. Exploring the richness of children's home lives can be a highly motivating stimulus for learning in school. With careful planning and classroom organisation, the multiplicity of ideas, issues and 'stories' that emanate from 30 individuals can be shared with all.
- Recognise that together with what parents and teachers know, children's own knowledge is core to the process of home–school knowledge exchange.

How do I do home–school knowledge exchange?

How can these principles be converted into effective practice? Let's look at some of the practical aspects of planning and conducting home–school knowledge exchange.

Build on what's already happening in school

It's often more effective to start with what is in place and develop this further, rather than opting immediately for groundbreaking innovations. Before our research started in the project schools, teachers were already developing links between children's out-of-school lives and their in-school learning. For example, we saw in Chapter 5 that the children in Geraint's school had previously been asked to keep a scrapbook of summer holiday events and bring these mementoes into class at the start of the school year. Although the response to this idea had been disappointing, it nevertheless contributed to the subsequent development of the shoebox activity in that school.

Build on activities

Rather than viewing an activity as a one-off event, it's often beneficial to follow through and capitalise on an initiative. Where success occurs, develop and consolidate what happens so that a momentum is achieved and home–school knowledge exchange becomes a two-way, iterative process. A good example of such a development was the sequence of activities around the trip to Cardiff Castle (Activity 5.4). As we saw, parents were invited to the pre-trip and post-trip writing workshops as well as accompanying their children to the castle itself.

Start with knowledge flowing from teachers to parents before tackling the home-to-school direction

It is relatively straightforward for teachers to inform parents about their instructional role, explaining what they teach and how they go about this. Indeed, a lot of schools already organise reading and writing workshops for parents of children starting in Reception class. Now that the literacy curriculum has become centrally prescribed and organised, teachers can articulate with professional confidence and clarity the content, methods, stages and even timing of literacy teaching in the classroom. What is much harder to achieve is helping parents to become confident about contributing to their children's literacy development, convincing them that they have a significant contribution to make to their children's learning. It is difficult to construct a framework that allows this fragile process to develop into an exchange of knowledge and expertise where the voice of individual parents and carers – including those who may feel very unconfident when talking to teachers – can be heard. Our experience suggests that the challenge of encouraging the flow of information from home to school will probably be more achievable once experience has been gained with school-to-home activities.

Put the child at the centre of activities

If well briefed, children are often the best ambassadors for new initiatives. A useful strategy, therefore, is to involve and inform children thoroughly before parents are contacted. We saw in Chapter 5 how Poppy's teacher developed a proactive strategy with her class to offset any parental worries or doubts about the activity she had planned. She did this by role-playing with the children what to say if their parents were quizzical or puzzled about what to do with the empty shoeboxes when they arrived home.

Use diverse means of communicating with parents

In our project we used an extensive range of strategies for communicating with parents. These included the use of video, photographs and innovative displays of children's work in accessible locations. If schools rely on a narrow range of methods for communicating with parents (typically involving the written word), it is possible that a correspondingly narrow range of parents will respond.

Take risks

Some of the most effective and creative responses occurred where the activities were novel and where positive outcomes were not guaranteed. The display of children's work in a local supermarket (Activity 4.2) is a good example of an activity where the outcomes were uncertain. The idea of exhibiting children's writing and other work in a commercial setting had not been tried out by the school before, and it was difficult to predict whether or not families would rise to the occasion. However, as we saw in Chapter 4, this casual 'drop in' event proved to be highly successful.

What are the likely challenges?

Creating closer connections between home and school is not always straightforward. Here we look at some of the challenges that can arise when putting home–school knowledge exchange into practice.

Hard-to-reach families – or hard-to-reach schools?

There is considerable variability – both within schools and between schools – in the extent to which parents engage with school. Headteachers in the project schools expressed their concern to us that not all parents would participate in school-based events to the extent that they, as headteachers, would like. As one headteacher put it:

> Eighty per cent . . . want to come in and want to be involved, but it's the small percentage who never come to school for anything . . . that's the challenge for the school.

Having described parents in terms of two 'camps' – those who come into school and those who don't – this headteacher noted that when home–school knowledge exchange activities were running in the school certain parents moved from the non-participating to the participating camp. An important issue here is that not all activities will appeal to all parents. This suggests that different approaches to engaging and valuing parents need to be developed if parents are going to move from the 'those who don't participate' to the 'those who do' camp.

The same headteacher also noted what was, for her, a surprising response to this research project from the parents in her school. She was taken aback by the enthusiastic and positive reaction we received when some parents were asked if we could interview them at home. This illustrates very well how parents *are* willing to get involved in issues and activities relating to their children's schooling as long as the activity suits their needs, interests and practical circumstances. This presents quite a challenge to the frequent description of some parents in official documents as being 'hard to reach'. Gill Crozier and Jane Davies have turned this idea around by applying it to schools rather than parents, asking whether, instead, certain schools are 'hard to reach' for parents (Crozier and Davies, 2007).

Respecting children's desire not to share their home lives

Valuing and incorporating children's home lives into the world of school can bring tangible benefits. We found that many children liked it when their teachers knew more about them, particularly when they got on well with their teacher and when they had developed a specific skill or interest they felt their teacher did not know about – such as dancing or kick boxing. We also noticed that Geraint's classmate Damien was slightly hurt when a supply teacher knew very little about his out-of-school life: 'She doesn't even know where my street is and all stuff like that.' However, it is important to consider whether there may be some aspects of home–school knowledge exchange activities with which children may not feel comfortable. For example, some of the activities involved children revealing personal details about themselves to their teacher and classmates. This might be a source of worry for some children for a number of reasons, such as what their teacher or their friends may think about their out-of-school interests or hobbies. Asking children to bring in artefacts from home can also present difficulties for some children. For example, when talking about the book sharing activity where children were asked to bring in books about animals (Activity 5.2), Zina's mother said: 'She wasn't happy, because she didn't have any books on animals to take in.'

Although we found that the number of children who did not engage with home–school knowledge exchange activities was small, it is worth mentioning the strategies developed by teachers to tackle this situation. Poppy's teacher, for example, paired up children who had not brought in items from home with those that had, so that all the children had access to artefacts they could discuss and write about. Another teacher found that rather than having a limited time-period during which children were expected to bring in material from home, an extended period of two weeks or so gave children time to see the sort of artefacts that their peers had collected and this tended to trigger their participation. In one school, the two boys who did not bring in artefacts were two of the first to bring in books for the book-sharing activity – some children are clearly more engaged by some activities than by others.

'We've tried it before and it doesn't work'

Don't be put off by comments such as, 'We've done that before and it doesn't work', or, 'It won't work in our school/with our parents.' The activities described in this book were developed in different schools in two cities. These schools were in a variety of locations and the parents and children came from diverse social backgrounds, including both the comparatively well-off and those where poverty and social deprivation were markedly apparent. So the provenance of the literacy activities is sound – each one has been field-tested with real teachers and real families.

However, it is important to highlight that each activity evolved from factors arising in specific schools and communities and was designed in response to particular issues raised by teachers and parents. As we saw earlier, teachers were asked at the start of the project about the information they would like to give to parents, and what they in turn would like to know about children's learning at home. In the same way, parents were asked what they would like to know about their children's learning at school. The activities described in Chapters 4 and 5 grew out of this initial mapping exercise and evolved as the project progressed. So, to a large extent, the activities were context-specific – specific to particular teachers and groups of parents, specific to particular issues in certain schools and in certain communities. Similarly, we need to stress that the activities described here are illustrative rather than exhaustive.

Does home–school knowledge exchange work in other curriculum subjects?

This book concentrates on literacy – all the activities and accounts of children's learning in school and at home have had literacy as a key focus. This raises the question as to whether learning in other subjects might equally benefit from home–school knowledge exchange. For a full account of how children's mathematical skills are enhanced by this process readers are advised to see our companion volume, *Improving Primary Mathematics: linking home and school*. It is also worth bearing in mind that some of the teachers who initially focused on literacy aspects of the activities described here subsequently applied these successfully to other subjects. For example we saw a teacher in Chapter 5 who used the contents of the children's shoeboxes in mathematics and history lessons.

What are the likely benefits?

We have already seen in Chapters 4 and 5 some of the positive effects that result when home and school literacy learning are brought together through home–school knowledge exchange. But it is worth reminding ourselves what those positive effects might be.

One of the most striking effects was the excitement and enthusiasm generated in the children when they were asked to bring into school some important part or parts of their home lives. For example, Amy's mother noted that 'She was quite excited about it beforehand – she talked about it quite a lot'. This was particularly significant, for Amy had been experiencing a difficult year at school until the time of this activity, and had not been particularly motivated in her approach to learning. Another parent was similarly pleased about how her child responded: Rebecca's mother talked about her child's obvious enjoyment when asked to share information about herself with her teacher and classmates through her shoebox, saying that: 'I think she likes to show people things about herself and I think she enjoys that. Yeah I think she really liked to do that.' When parents, siblings or other family members had an opportunity to share their expertise in school via, for example, a writing workshop, children responded very enthusiastically to such opportunities to work alongside them in class. Damien, for example, said: '[That was] really good, because I know he's my uncle. And one thing as well, he's a really good drawer!'

Parents also appreciated the way school-to-home activities allowed them to see their children in action in the classroom. When Seren's mother thought back to the video of Seren's literacy lesson, she said:

> Yes, I thought it was good. It's nice to see your children in a different light, because you always say, don't you, 'I'd love to be a fly on the wall.' No, I thought that was good

Parents and children also expressed their pleasure in seeing school work exhibited in a local supermarket. As we saw in Chapter 4, having their work displayed in a public place gave the children and their parents a real sense of pride.

The teachers and headteachers were also notably positive about the activities that had been developed in their schools. Teachers acknowledged the benefits of the home–school knowledge exchange activities in terms of increasing their knowledge of the children's out-of-school lives. One teacher noted: 'I know it sounds really sad to say, but I don't have time to ask them what they do out of school.' She added that she had found out much about children's interests and activities through the 'All About Me' shoebox activity. Poppy's teacher observed that Harry, a pupil in her class, had responded well to the shoebox activity where children were encouraged to bring in items to stimulate story writing. When accounting for his enjoyment of this activity she referred to the degree of choice and independence the children had over the content of their writing, 'Certainly he really enjoyed things like that box project, where he had control over what he was going to write about.' The same teacher noted that the process of writing a story based on their shoebox items and then preparing the story for publication in a class collection of stories helped the children to understand the various stages involved: 'I think that helped them see writing as a process as well, because they hand-wrote them originally and then they selected the piece and typed it up with adult help and help from peers.'

The headteacher of the school where children and parents visited Cardiff Castle and collaborated in writing workshops noted the effects on the children: '[They] just absolutely loved it and the work they produced, oh, it was a delight, really was.' Clearly the level of the children's enjoyment together with the impact this had on children's literacy work were key factors emerging from this particular home–school knowledge exchange activity. The same headteacher summarised the effect of the project on the school's work with children and parents when she commented:

> And I think it's given them [parents] a better insight into what goes on in the classroom, ways in which they can help us in school, ways in which they can help their children at home. It's had a very, very positive impact.

The above comments are indicative of the beneficial impact of knowledge exchange activities on schools and families. Children, parents and teachers not only enjoyed participating in this style of working, they also valued the contribution it made to children's literacy learning.

Unforeseen spin-offs

If an idea is seen to be good then it will probably be extended or developed. One example of this occurred in the school where children collected artefacts in shoeboxes to support their creative writing. In the same school, the Special Educational Needs Coordinator recognised the potential of this activity for providing support for children transferring from infant to junior school. She thought that filling shoeboxes with important artefacts from home would help these children introduce themselves to their new teachers. Initially, it was planned that only children with special needs would get involved, but it soon became apparent that many children would benefit, so this was quickly transformed into an activity for all the children transferring from Key Stage 1 to Key Stage 2.

In Parveen's school, where parents as well as siblings had participated in a writing workshop, the use of older brothers and sisters had been so successful that their teacher continued to use this as a reward – i.e. the opportunity to visit other classes as helpers. This activity had the unexpected effect of raising the self-esteem of older siblings who had been used as helpers with their younger brothers and sisters – children who might not usually have been given such responsibility and invited to act in this helping capacity.

Conclusion

This book has demonstrated that children's literacy learning will be enhanced if ways can be found of bringing together the knowledge and experience that are present both at home and at school. We are confident that the examples provided here will enable readers to develop courses of action that match their professional or personal contexts, and that the outcomes will be as effective, creative and enjoyable as those we have described here.

Appendix: The Home School Knowledge Exchange Project

The Home School Knowledge Exchange Project was funded by the Economic and Social Research Council (ESRC) between 2001 and 2005. The project was part of a large research programme called the Teaching and Learning Research Programme (TLRP). The TLRP is concerned with improving outcomes for learners in a very wide range of UK contexts across the lifecourse.

The Home School Knowledge Exchange Project was based on the assumption that both parents and teachers have knowledge that is relevant to enhancing children's learning, but that this knowledge is often poorly communicated and under-utilised. The overall aim of the project was to develop, understand and evaluate ways in which pupil attainment and learning disposition could be enhanced by a process of knowledge exchange between parents and teachers, which also involved children themselves.

There were three strands to the project, with the following foci:

- developing literacy at Key Stage 1
- developing numeracy at Key Stage 2
- facilitating transfer between Key Stage 2 and 3.

Below we provide details of the literacy strand of the project.

Literacy strand: design

Within the literacy strand, four schools actively participated in the project ('action schools'). In these schools the activities described in Chapters 4 and 5 were developed and put into practice. Two of the schools were in Bristol and two in Cardiff. Within each city, one school had a relatively high proportion of pupils eligible for free school meals while the other had a relatively low proportion. We tried to ensure that the schools' intakes reflected Bristol's and Cardiff's ethnic diversity. In addition, the Cardiff action school with a low number of pupils eligible for free meals was a Welsh-medium school where the curriculum at Key Stage 1 was taught wholly in Welsh.

A set of four schools matched to the action schools was also recruited to the project. These schools did not carry out any activities but provided the opportunity for quantitative comparisons to be made of the pupils' learning outcomes.

Literacy activities

Three teacher-researchers were seconded to the project between 2001 and 2004, one for each strand. The role of the teacher-researcher in the literacy strand was to work closely with teachers and parents in the action schools developing literacy-related home–school knowledge exchange activities and supporting their implementation.

The project team felt it was important not to impose ideas upon the participants. The first step, then, was a mapping exercise whereby the current state of home–school interchange and the knowledge exchange needs of those involved were investigated. Headteachers and teachers in the four literacy strand action schools were interviewed and parents were sent questionnaires (translated into home languages where appropriate) and invited to take part in discussion groups (some of the outcomes of this mapping are described at the start of Chapters 4 and 5).

The literacy teacher-researcher focused her work on one class in each of the four schools. At the beginning of the project the children in these classes were starting Year 1, and they continued to be the focus of the project's work during Year 2.

Evaluating the project's impact

Other members of the project team carried out work designed to evaluate and understand the impact of the knowledge exchange activities on the children, their families and their schools. A range of different methods was used for this.

Quantitative assessments of all the children in the action and comparison classes were carried out at the start of Year 1, the start of Year 2 and the end of Year 2. The assessments had three main components – a standardised assessment of the children's attainment in literacy and numeracy, an assessment of their learning disposition, and an assessment of their self-efficacy in literacy. The children's attainment in literacy and numeracy was assessed using the Performance Indicators in Primary Schools (PIPS) tests produced by the Curriculum, Evaluation and Management Centre at Durham University. In the Welsh-medium schools, the attainment assessments were in Welsh and were administered by a Welsh speaking teacher. The children's learning dispositions were assessed using a junior version of the 'Effective Lifelong Learning Inventory' developed at the University of Bristol (Deakin Crick et al., 2004). The children's subject-related self-efficacy was assessed using questionnaires devised by the project. These assessments of learning disposition and self-efficacy were administered in both English and Welsh in the Welsh medium schools, since the majority of pupils spoke English as their home language. A small number of the youngest pupils for whom English was an additional language in the other schools had the efficacy and disposition tests read to them in their home language to obviate difficulties with understanding.

In each action class, further exploration of a mainly qualitative nature was conducted with six 'target' families. Six pupils (a higher attaining boy and girl, a medium attaining boy and girl and a lower attaining boy and girl) were chosen through stratified random selection. Their parents were invited to participate in this part of the research, mostly by phone, although a few were approached directly in the playground at school, or at home. All but two agreed and reserves were approached in these cases. Interviews with the parents and children in the target families were used to explore thoughts and feelings about literacy and to monitor responses to the knowledge exchange activities retrospectively. The final set of interviews included the use of photographs taken during the activities to prompt stimulated recall. The families also made videos of literacy events taking place at home, and the target pupils were observed in literacy lessons at school.

More prolonged and intensive explorations were pursued with a number of families selected from amongst the targets. These case studies allowed a more detailed investigation with those involved. A variety of techniques was used here, including diaries made by the participants (both written and photographic), videos, observation, informal chats, and drawing and model making with some of the children. The accounts given in Chapters 2 and 3 of literacy learning at home and at school are based on some of this case study data.

During the course of the project, teachers and headteachers were interviewed individually and informal discussions were also held from time to time. The interviews with the teachers included their views about literacy learning and teaching, their feelings about involving parents, their responses to the activities and their appraisals of the target children. The sustainability of knowledge exchange activities was a particular feature of the discussions with headteachers.

Further information

Further information about the Home School Knowledge Exchange project can be found at www.home–school-learning.org.uk.

Further information about the Teaching and Learning Research Programme can be found at www.tlrp.org.

References

Clough, P. and Nutbrown, C. (2002) *A Student's Guide to Methodology: justifying enquiry*, London: Sage.

Crozier, G. and Davies, J. (2007) 'Hard to reach parents or hard to reach schools? A discussion of home–school relations, with particular reference to Bangladeshi and Pakistani parents', *British Educational Research Journal*, 33: 3.

Deakin Crick, R., Broadfoot, P. and Claxton, G. (2004) 'Developing an effective lifelong learning inventory: the ELLI project', *Assessment in Education*, 11: 248–272.

Dombey, H. (1995) 'Reading: what children need to learn and how teachers can help them', in C. Gains and D. Wray (eds) *Reading: issues and directions*, Stafford: NASEN Enterprises.

Greenhough, P. and Hughes, M. (1999) 'Encouraging conversing: trying to change what parents do when their children read with them', *Reading*, 33: 98–105.

Marsh, J. (2003) 'One way traffic? Connections between literacy practices at home and in the nursery', *British Educational Research Journal*, 29: 369–382.

Marsh, J. and Thompson, P. (2001) 'Parental involvement in literacy development: using media texts', *Journal of Research in Reading*, 24: 266–278.

QCA (2003) *Foundation Stage Profile Handbook*. Online. Available at www.qca.org.uk/downloads/5824_handbook_web.pdf.

Wolfendale, S. (2004) 'Getting the balance right: towards partnership in assessing children's development and educational achievement', DfES discussion paper for TeacherNet. Online. Available at www.teachernet.gov.uk/docbank/index.cfm?id=7302.

Index